Vedânta Philosophy

How to be a Yogi

&

Five Lectures

On

Reincarnation

By

Swami Abhedananda

Edited by Dr. Jane Ma'ati Smith

ISBN #1438251378 and EAN-13 # 9781438251370

How to be a Yogi
Vedânta Philosophy
By
Swami Abhedananda
Edited by Dr. Jane Ma'ati Smith

CONTENTS

For the ultimate in deeply transformative Chakra meditation
CD's and MP3's visit
www.chakrahealingsounds.com

Swami Abhedananda

Swami Abhedananda was born on October 2, 1866 as Kaliprasad Chandra. He was a direct disciple of Sri Ramakrishna. After the death of Sri Ramakrishna, he formally became a Sanyasi, and became known as "Swami Abhedananda".

During his life, he traveled extensively throughout India, depending entirely on alms. During this time he met many famous sages like Paohari Baba, Trailanga Swami and Swami Bhaskaranand. He travelled to the sources of the Ganges and the Yamuna rivers, and meditated in the Himalayas. Swami Vivekananda asked him to take the message of Vedanta to the West; he went to United States in 1897, and preached the messages of Vedanta and the teachings of his Guru for about 25 years, with great success. He returned to India in 1921.

In 1922, at the age of 56, he crossed the Himalayas on foot and reached Tibet, where he studied Buddhist philosophy and Lamaism. At the Hemis Monastery, he discovered a manuscript on the "lost years" of Jesus Christ, which he incorporated in his book "Swami Abhedananda's Journey Into Kashmir & Tibet". He formed the 'Ramakrishna Vedanta Society' in Kolkata India in 1923, which is now known as Ramakrishna Vedanta Math. In 1924, he established Ramakrishna Vedanta Math in Darjeeling in West Bengal, India. Swami Abhedananda died on September 8, 1939.

How to be a Yogi

Preface

THE Vedânta Philosophy includes the different branches of the Science of Yoga. Four of these have already been treated at length by the Swâmi Vivekananda in his works on "Râja Yoga," "Karma Yoga," "Bhakti Yoga," and "Jnâna Yoga"; but there existed no short and consecutive survey of the science as a whole. It is to meet this need that the present volume has been written. In an introductory chapter are set forth the true province of religion and the full significance of the word "spirituality" as it is understood in India. Next follows a comprehensive definition of the term "Yoga," with short chapters on each of the five paths to which it is applied, and their respective practices. An exhaustive exposition of the Science of Breathing and its bearing on the highest spiritual development shows the fundamental physiological principles on which the whole training of Yoga is based; while a concluding chapter, under the title "Was Christ a Yogi?" makes plain the direct relation existing between the lofty teachings of Vedânta and the religious faiths of the West. An effort has been made, so far as possible, to keep the text free from technical and Sanskrit terms; and the work should therefore prove of equal value to the student of Oriental thought and to the general reader as yet unfamiliar with this, one of the greatest philosophical systems of the world.

Introduction

TRUE religion is extremely practical; it is, indeed, based entirely upon practice, and not upon theory or speculation of any kind, for religion begins only where theory ends. Its object is to mould the character, unfold the divine nature of the soul, and make it possible to live on the spiritual plane, its ideal being the realization of Absolute Truth and the manifestation of Divinity in the actions of the daily life.

Spirituality does not depend upon the reading of Scriptures, or upon learned interpretations of Sacred Books, or upon fine theological discussions, but upon the realization of unchangeable Truth. In India a man is called truly spiritual or religious not because he has written some book, not because he possesses the gift of oratory and can preach eloquent sermons, but because he expresses divine powers through his words and deeds. A thoroughly illiterate man can attain to the highest state of spiritual perfection without going to any school or university, and without reading any Scripture, if he can conquer his animal nature by realizing his true Self and its relation to the universal Spirit; or, in other words, if he can attain to the knowledge of that Truth which dwells within him, and which is the same as the Infinite Source of existence, intelligence, and bliss. He who has mastered all the Scriptures, philosophies, and sciences, may be regarded by society as an intellectual giant; yet he cannot be equal to that unlettered man who, having realized the eternal Truth, has become one with it, who sees God everywhere, and who lives on this earth as an embodiment of Divinity.

The writer had the good fortune to be acquainted with such a divine man in India. His name was Râmakrishna. He never went to any school, neither had he read any of the Scriptures, philosophies, or scientific treatises of the world, yet he had reached perfection by realizing God through the practice of Yoga. Hundreds of men and women came to see him and were spiritually awakened and uplifted by the divine powers, which this illiterate man possessed. To-day he is revered and worshipped by thousands all over India as is Jesus the Christ in Christendom. He could expound with extraordinary clearness the subtlest problems of philosophy or of science, and answer the most intricate questions of clever theologians in such a masterly way as to dispel all doubts concerning the matter in hand. How could he do this without reading books? By his wonderful insight into the true nature of things, and by that Yoga power which made him directly perceive things which cannot be revealed by the senses. His spiritual eyes were open; his sight could penetrate through the thick veil of ignorance that hangs before the vision of ordinary mortals, and which prevents them from knowing that which exists beyond the range of sense perception.

These powers begin to manifest in the soul that is awakened to the ultimate Reality of the universe. It is then that the sixth sense of direct perception of higher truths develops and frees it from dependence upon the sense powers. This sixth sense or spiritual eye is latent in each individual, but it opens in a few only among millions, and they are known as Yogis. With the vast majority it is in a rudimentary state, covered by a thick veil. When, however, through the practice of Yoga it unfolds in a man, he becomes conscious of the higher invisible realms and of everything that exists on the soul plane. Whatever he says harmonizes with the sayings and writings of all the great Seers of Truth of every age and clime. He does not study books; he has no need to do so, for he knows all that the human intellect can conceive. He can grasp the purport of a book without reading its text; he also understands how much the human mind can express through words, and he is familiar with that which is beyond thoughts and which consequently can never be expressed by words.

Before arriving at such spiritual illumination he goes through divers stages of mental and spiritual evolution, and in consequence knows all that can be experienced by a human intellect. He does not, however, care to remain confined within the limit of sense perception, and is not contented with the intellectual apprehension of relative reality, but his sole aim is to enter into the realm of the Absolute, which is the beginning and end of phenomenal objects and of relative knowledge. Thus striving for the realization of the highest, he does not fail to collect all relative knowledge pertaining to the world of phenomena that comes in his way, as he marches on toward his destination, the unfoldment of his true Self.

Our true Self is all-knowing by its nature. It is the source of infinite knowledge within us. Being bound by the limitations of time, space, and causation, we cannot express all the powers that we possess in reality. The higher we rise above these limiting conditions, the more we can manifest the divine qualities of omniscience and omnipotence. If, on the contrary, we keep our minds fixed upon phenomena and devote the whole of our energy to acquiring knowledge dependent entirely upon sense perceptions, shall we ever reach the end of phenomenal knowledge, shall we ever be able to know the real nature of the things of this universe? No; because the senses cannot lead us beyond the superficial appearance of sense objects. In order to go deeper in the realm of the invisible we invent instruments, and with their help we are able to penetrate a little further; but these instruments, again, have their limit. After using one kind of instrument, we become dissatisfied with the results and search for some other which may reveal more and more, and thus we struggle on, discovering at each step how poor and helpless are the sense powers in the path of the knowledge of the Absolute. At last we are driven to the conclusion that any instrument, no matter how fine, can never help us to realize that which is beyond the reach of sense-perception, intellect, and thought.

So, even if we could spend the whole of our time and energy in studying phenomena, we shall never arrive at any satisfactory result or be able to see things as they are in reality. The knowledge of to-day, gained by the help of certain instruments, will be the ignorance of tomorrow, if we get better instruments. The knowledge of last year is already the ignorance of the present year; the knowledge of this century will be ignorance in the light of the discoveries of a new century.

The span of one human life is, therefore, too short to even attempt to acquire a correct knowledge of all things existing on the phenomenal plane. The life-time of hundreds of thousands of generations, nay, of all humanity, seems too short, when we consider the infinite variety to be found in the universe, and the countless number of objects that will have to be known before we can reach the end of knowledge. If a man could live a million years, keeping his senses in perfect order during that long period, and could spend every moment in studying nature and in diligently endeavoring to learn every minute detail of phenomenal objects, would his search after knowledge be fulfilled at the expiration of that time? Certainly not; he would want still more time, a finer power of perception, a keener intellect, a subtler understanding; and then he might say, as did Sir Isaac Newton after a life of tireless research, "I have collected only pebbles on the shore of the ocean of knowledge." If a genius like Newton could not even reach the edge of the water of that ocean, how can we expect to cross the vast expanse from shore to shore in a few brief years? Thousands of generations have passed away, thousands will pass, yet must the knowledge regarding the phenomena of the universe remain imperfect. Veil after veil may be removed, but veil after veil will remain behind. This was understood by the Yogis and Seers of Truth in India, who said: "Innumerable are the branches of knowledge, but short is our time and many are the obstacles in the way; therefore wise men should first struggle to know that which is highest."

Here the question arises: Which is the highest knowledge? This question is as old as history; it has puzzled the minds of the philosophers, scientists, and scholars of all ages and all countries. Some have found an answer to it, others have not. The same question was voiced in ancient times by Socrates, when he went to the Delphic oracle and asked: "Of all knowledge which is the highest?" To which came the answer, "Know thyself."

We read in one of the Upanishads that a great thinker, after studying all the philosophies and sciences known at that time, came to a Seer of Truth and said: "Sir, I am tired of this lower knowledge that can be gained from books or through the study of the world of phenomena; it no longer satisfies me, for science cannot reveal the ultimate Truth; I wish to know that which is the highest. Is there anything by knowing which I can know the reality of the universe?"

The sage replied: "Yes, there is; and that knowledge is the highest, by knowing which you can know the true nature of everything in the universe." And he continued, "Know thyself. If thou canst learn the true nature of thine own self, thou wilt know the reality of the universe. In thy true Self thou wilt find the Eternal Truth, the Infinite Source of all phenomena. By knowing this thou wilt know God and His whole creation." As by knowing the chemical properties of one drop of water, we know the properties of all water wherever it appears, so by knowing who and what we are in reality, we shall realize the final Truth. Man is the epitome of the universe. That which exists in the macrocosm is to be found in the microcosm. Therefore the knowledge of one's true Self is the highest of all knowledge. Our real Self is divine and one with God. This may seem to us at present a mere theory, but the nearer we approach the ultimate Truth, the more clearly shall we understand that it is not a theory but a fact, that now we are dreaming in the sleep of ignorance and fancying ourselves this or that particular person. But as all experience gained in dreams afterwards appears of little consequence; so, waking up from this sleep, we shall find that the knowledge of phenomenal nature, upon which we place so much value at present, is of little importance. We shall then realize that all research in the various branches of science depends upon Self-knowledge, and that Self-knowledge is the foundation upon which the structure of phenomenal knowledge is built.

Knowledge of the Self or Âtman is therefore the highest of all. It is the ideal of the Science of Yoga, and should be the aim of our life. We should hold it as our first duty to acquire this Self-knowledge before we try to know anything concerning the objects of sense-perception. How can we gain it? Not from books, not through the study of external phenomena, but by studying our own nature, and by practicing the different branches of Yoga.

What is Yoga?

IN all the Sacred Writings of the world as well as in the lives of the inspired teachers, prophets, saints, and Seers of Truth, we find frequent descriptions of miraculous events and powers, which, admitting a certain measure of exaggeration, must still have had some foundation in fact. We, indeed, know that from time immemorial in every age and in every country there have arisen among the different nations persons who could read the thoughts of others, who could foresee and could prophesy that which afterwards came to pass; but most of these people did not understand the causes of their own peculiar gifts, and tried to explain them by attributing them to the influence of external Beings, whom they called by various names--gods, angels, good or evil spirits.

Some among them even fancied that they were especially chosen to be the instruments of these higher powers and sought to be worshipped as the elect of God or of their particular deity, just as the leaders of certain sects in this country to-day desire to be adored by their followers. In some instances, those who possessed these unusual powers were looked upon as divine exceptions, as Jesus by the Christians, Mahomet by the Mahometans, and Buddha by the Buddhists. Others again were condemned as sorcerers or witches, and the fear aroused by such persecutions led to the secret practice of divers methods which resulted in still further extraordinary manifestations.

These methods were never written down, but were passed orally from the master to the disciple, who in turn carefully guarded them as sacred mysteries. This is the reason why among ancient nations there grew up so many secret societies, the object of which was to develop certain powers through various kinds of discipline and practices. The Egyptians, the Essenes, Gnostics, Manicheans, Neo-Platonists, and the Christian mystics of the middle ages all had their secret organizations, and some of them still exist, as, for example, the Masonic Lodge. None of the members of these societies ever gave out their secret instructions, nor did they write any books offering a logical or scientific explanation of their practices. Therefore, while there were some among them who advanced far in the attainment of higher powers, the unusual manifestations resulting therefrom were never understood by Western nations, neither were they generalized into a system or science.

In ancient India, on the contrary, as there was no fear of persecution, the case was altogether different. Every Hindu was obliged, as a part of his religious duty, to develop through daily practice certain powers and to strive to attain to the realization of higher truths. In the streets, on the market-place, in the courts, and on the battle-field were many who had not only reached such realization, but who had carefully classified their experiences and discovered those laws which govern our higher nature and upon which was gradually built up the profound Science of Yoga.

Thus we see that this science, like all others, was based on experience; while the method used in it was the same as that employed by modern science in making all its discoveries of natural law--the method of observation and experiment. This method is regarded in the West as a distinctly modern innovation, but as a matter of fact it was adopted in India in very ancient times by the "Rishis," or Seers of Truth. Through the process of close observation and constant experiment they discovered the finer forces of nature, as also the laws that govern our physical, mental, and spiritual being. The truths thus gained through their own experience and investigations, they wrote down in books, preached in public, and expounded to their pupils. Before, however, they affirmed anything about the nature of the soul or God, they had realized it. Before they asked a disciple to practice anything they had practiced it themselves, and had obtained definite results from that practice.

In this way, as the outcome of ages of research in the realms of nature, carried on by a succession of earnest seekers after light, there grew up in India various systems of science, philosophy, psychology, metaphysics, and religion, both speculative and practical, which were grouped under the one common name, "Aryan Religion." The term "religion" was used to include all, because at no epoch in India has religion been separated from these different branches or from the general conduct of every-day existence; and the methods by which these scientific truths were applied in the daily life of an individual to further his spiritual development, were called by the general term "Yoga."

"Yoga" is a Sanskrit word commonly used to signify the practical side of religion; and the first concern of the training for which it stands, is to enforce proper obedience to the laws of our moral and physical nature, upon which depend the attainment of perfect health and of moral and spiritual perfection. In Western countries the word has been grossly misunderstood and misused by many writers, who have employed it in the sense of jugglery, hypnotism, trickery, and fraud. Whenever people hear the word "Yogi," which signifies one who practices Yoga, they think of some kind of juggler, or charlatan, or identify him with a fakir or one who practices black magic. The Theosophists have been more or less responsible for this abuse of the term; but those who have studied the Sacred Books of India, as, for instance, the Bhagavad Gita or Song Celestial, as Sir Edwin Arnold calls it in his translation, will remember that each chapter of that Celestial Song is devoted to some kind of "Yoga," or method of realizing the Ultimate Truth and of attaining the highest wisdom; and that a "Yogi" is one who through various practices reaches the highest ideal of religion. This highest ideal, according to the Bhagavad Gita, is the union of the individual soul with the Universal Spirit.

Hindu writers, however, have used the word "Yoga" in various other senses. I will mention a few of them in order to give some

14

conception of the vastness of the field covered by this term. First, "Yoga" means the union of two external objects. Second, the mixing of one thing with another. Third, the interrelation of the causes which produce a common effect. Fourth, the orderly equipment of a soldier or of any person in any profession. Fifth, the application, discrimination, and reasoning that is necessary for the discovery of a certain truth. Sixth, that power of sound which makes it convey a specific idea. Seventh, the preservation of what one possesses. Eighth, the transformation of one thing into another. Ninth, the union of one soul with another or with the universal Spirit. Tenth, the flowing of a thought current towards an object. Eleventh, the restraint of all thought action through concentration and meditation. Thus we see how many different branches of art, science, psychology, philosophy, and religion are included in the various definitions of this one word. It seems, indeed, in its scope and range to take in every department of nature. If, however, we consider the literal meaning of the word, we shall more easily understand why it is so all-inclusive.

It is derived from the Sanskrit root "Yuj," which means to join. The English word "yoke" also comes from the same root. Originally the literal signification of the two words was almost the same. The root-verb "Yuj" signifies to join oneself to something, or to harness oneself for some task. Thus in its primary meaning it conveys the same idea of preparing for hard work as the common English expressions "to go into harness," or "to buckle to." The effort required is mental or physical, according to the object in view. If the object be the acquirement of perfect health or longevity, then the effort of both mind and body to accomplish this through certain practices is called "Yoga." So is it again if the object be the development of psychic powers. The same word is used likewise to indicate the mental training necessary for the attainment of self-control, of the union of the individual soul with God, of divine communion or of spiritual perfection. Volumes upon volumes have been written in India describing the different branches and methods of this applied science of "Yoga," and the various ideals that can be attained through its practice; also what qualifications fit a beginner for undertaking any of these methods, what stages he must pass through in order to reach the goal, what obstacles stand in the way, and how they can be overcome.

Patience and perseverance are absolutely necessary for any one who desires to enter upon the path of Yoga; those who are not patient cannot hope to arrive at true realization. Those, again, who take it up out of curiosity or through an impulse of temporary enthusiasm, must not expect to get results, and must not blame the teacher for their failure to do so, since the fault is entirely their own. The same teachings, when carried out with understanding and in the right spirit, will bring wonderful results. They will only come, however, to the student who follows strictly the instructions of a living master, who will direct him in the practice of both physical and mental exercises.

Aspirants to the study of Yoga can be divided into three classes: First, those who are born Yogis. There are some who, having practiced Yoga in a previous incarnation, come here as awakened souls, and as such manifest remarkable powers from their very childhood. Their natural tendency is to lead a pure life, for right living and right thinking are their sole concern, and they possess wonderful powers of self-control and of concentration. Sense pleasures and those things which fascinate the ordinary mind have no charm for them. Even when they are surrounded by all the comforts of life and have every material resource at their command, they yet feel like strangers in a strange land. Few there are who can understand properly the mental condition of these characters. Physicians may be brought to them, but medical treatment may only make them worse; the writer knows of cases where harm has been done in this way. By the law of attraction, however, they are bound to be drawn sooner or later into the companionship of some Yogi. Here they find exactly what their inner nature has been craving, and at once they feel happy and at home. The instructions of the Yogi appeal to their minds; they begin the practice of Yoga under his direction, and proving easy and natural to them, they soon obtain excellent results. Thus from youth they take up the thread of the practice at the very

16

point where they dropped it in their past existence; and through a firm determination to overcome all obstacles in their way, they progress rapidly and gradually attain to the highest ideal of spiritual life. Nothing in the world can prevent their onward march, so intense and strong is their longing for realization.

The second class includes those who are born as half-awakened souls. In need of further experience, they go through various paths without finding the right one. They take each new step tentatively, and in this constant experimenting, they waste a great deal of energy and a large portion of their lives. If such partially awakened souls, following out a tendency created in their previous existence, have the good fortune to come in contact with a Yogi and take up the practice of Yoga, they may, through perseverance and earnestness, achieve much in this life, although they will necessarily advance more slowly in the path of spirituality than those who belong to the first class.

In the third class are to be found all those unawakened souls who begin their search after Truth and the practice of Yoga for the first time in this life. Even from childhood they are irresistibly drawn towards sense objects and sense pleasures; and if they take up the practice of Yoga, they find great difficulty in following its teachings and meet numerous obstacles along the way. Their environment is not favorable for the practice, and even when they try, they cannot easily conquer it. Their health is not good, their mind is scattered, and they suffer from various kinds of disease and mental disturbance. They also lack determination, find it well-nigh impossible to control the senses, and have to fight hard to adjust their mode of living to the new requirements. With so much to contend against they naturally obtain but small results even after long practice. If, however, such persons can persevere and strengthen their wills through a slow and regular practice of Hatha Yoga, struggling manfully to overcome the many obstacles in their way by the practice of breathing exercises and by following the directions of a competent teacher, who understands them, they may in this life be able to control in a large measure their physical health and acquire a certain amount of Yoga power. Hatha Yoga is especially useful for this class of aspirants. Through the practice of breathing exercises they will gradually gain control over their bodies, and will, in course of time, be prepared for the study of Râja Yoga, which will arouse the powers latent in their souls.

Hatha Yoga

HATHA YOGA is that branch of the Science of Yoga which teaches how to conquer hunger, thirst, and sleep; how to overcome the effects of heat and cold; how to gain perfect health and cure disease without using drugs; how to arrest the untimely decay of the body resulting from the waste of vital energy; how to preserve youth even at the age of one hundred without having a single hair turn grey, and how thus to prolong life in this body for an indefinite period. Anyone who practices it will in the course of time acquire marvellous powers; powers indeed, which must dumbfound a psychologist or anatomist.

A few years ago a Hatha Yogi was brought to England. Although in middle life he looked like a boy of eighteen. Not only was his physical condition perfect, but through practice he had mastered eighty-four postures of the body. He could bend his limbs in so astonishing a way that it seemed as if his joints must be unattached, while his bones were as though made of some elastic substance. Many English physicians and surgeons came to see him and were amazed at the extraordinary positions of his limbs. They brought a skeleton and tried to fix its bones in the same positions, but could not do so without breaking them. Afterwards they reached the conclusion that if the bones were once fixed in those positions the limbs would be unfitted for any kind of work. Yet the example of the Yogi openly contradicted their statements. His limbs were strong and of good use to him in every possible way. He could walk, lift heavy weights, and move about with absolute ease. The writer himself saw him in India, and also other Hatha Yogis who could accomplish equally wonderful feats. The primary object of these various postures described in Hatha

Yoga is to gain control over the involuntary muscles of the body, which is impossible to the ordinary man. We all possess this power latent within us, but the Hatha Yogis were the first to discover a scientific method by which it could be developed.

All Hatha Yogis eat very little, but they can also go entirely without food for days and even for months, and succeed in conquering sleep. The author knew of one who had not slept for twelve years, and who was nevertheless in perfect health. He has also seen a Hatha Yogi who usually ate, for instance, a piece of unleavened bread in twenty-four hours, and who refused to wear warm clothing in the coldest winter weather, and yet who voluntarily worked hard as a street laborer without showing the least sign of fatigue. It may seem impossible to the majority of people, who have made themselves such slaves to sleep and food as to imagine that if they do not sleep eight or nine hours out of the twenty-four and eat pounds of flesh, they cannot live. Hatha Yogis are the living contradictions of such opinions. Perhaps the reader is familiar with the account of that Yogi who was buried alive for forty days in an hermetically sealed box, with a guard of English officers to watch the spot night and day. During these forty days the Yogi could neither eat, sleep, nor breathe, yet at their expiration he was brought back to consciousness without any ill effects and he lived for many years.

Then again these same Yogis who do not eat, sleep, or drink for a long period, can, if they wish, eat as much as ten persons at one time without suffering any unpleasant consequences. Of course they do not eat any kind of meat. They digest their food consciously, as it were. They claim that by a third eye they can, so to speak, see what is going on in their internal organs. Why should this seem incredible to us when the discovery of the Roentgen rays has proved everything to be transparent?

Some of the Hatha Yogis have extraordinary eyesight. They can not only perceive objects at a great distance, but can also see clearly in complete darkness, even being able to pick up a pin from the floor without the least glimmer of ordinary light to guide them. This will not appear so strange when we remember that there is invisible light in the atmosphere of a perfectly dark room. If we can learn to use this atmospheric light, imperceptible to the common eye, and can develop our eyesight, there is no reason why we should not see things in the dark. The Yogis understand this and know the method by which the power of eyesight can be developed. As regards distinguishing objects at a great distance, this is not so difficult to believe since we know that there are persons living, not Yogis, who can see the moons of Jupiter without the help of any instrument.

This branch of optical science in Hatha Yoga is called in Sanskrit "Trâtaka" Yoga. It teaches, among other things, how, through gazing on one object and at the same time performing certain special breathing exercises, many optical maladies can be cured as well as the power of sight strengthened. The authentic records of Hatha Yogis vouch for the fact that it produces many beneficial effects when properly practiced under the direction of a competent master of Hatha Yoga.

A Yogi who is expert in this science of optics can fascinate or madden another by his optical powers. The process of hypnotism or mesmerism verifies this claim. A Yogi can likewise read the thoughts of another by looking at his eyes; for according to the Yogi the eye is the index of the mind. Here it may be asked, how do the Yogis acquire these powers? They do not get them from outside. These powers are dormant in every individual, and through practice the Yogis bring them out. They say: "Whatever exists in the universe (the macrocosm) exists also in the human body (the microcosm)." That is, the finer forces exist potentially in our own organism, and if we study our nature carefully we shall be able to know all the forces and the laws which govern the universe.

Hatha Yoga, again, teaches the cure of disease through breathing exercises and the regulation of diet and of the general habits of the daily life. But it does not claim that physical health is the same as spirituality. On the contrary, it tells us that if a healthy body were a sign of spirituality, then wild animals and savages who enjoy perfect health would be exceedingly spiritual; yet they are not, as we know. The principal idea of these Yogis is that physical maladies are obstacles in the path of spiritual progress, while a healthy body furnishes one of the most favorable conditions for the realization of the highest spiritual truths in this life. Those who do not possess good health should, therefore, begin to practice Hatha Yoga.

In the practice of Hatha Yoga strict dietetic rules must be observed. Anything that is sharp, sour, pungent, or hot, like mustard, liquors, fish, flesh of animals, curd, buttermilk, oil cakes, carrots, onions, and garlic should not be eaten. Food, again, which, having been once cooked, has grown cold and been rewarmed, should be avoided; as should also excess of salt or acidity, or that which is hard to digest. Rice, barley, wheat, milk, sugar, honey, and butter are good for a Hatha Yogi's diet. The manner in which Americans live in hotels and boarding-houses, where the food is often unclean, is far from favorable to this practice. Food cooked for hundreds of people in a restaurant cannot be equally good for all and may easily cause disease. Those who wish to enjoy perfect health must be careful about what they eat; they must also observe all the laws of hygiene regarding cleanliness of the body, fresh air, and pure water. They should not live in over-heated houses; neither should they indulge in artificial stimulants, especially beer, wine, and coffee. The habit of excessive coffee-drinking is a serious menace to the American nation. Many people are already suffering from nervous prostration as a result of indulgence in this direction, and there are very few cases in which the nervous system will not be affected by it to some extent.

He who wishes to practice Hatha Yoga should first of all find a Hatha Yogi teacher, who has perfect control over his physical body; and having found him, he should lead a life in strict accord with his instructions. He should live in a secluded spot and where the changes of weather are neither sudden nor extreme. He should be a rigid vegetarian and abstain from all kinds of drinks that stimulate the system. He should never fill the stomach with a large quantity of food. He should observe the moral laws and practice absolute continence. He should learn to control his senses, keep his body clean, and purify his mind by arousing feelings of kindness and love towards all living creatures.

The beginner in this branch of Yoga should gradually conquer the different postures of the body and limbs. These postures are called in Sanskrit *Asâna*. There are altogether eighty-four of them described in the science of Hatha Yoga. Each of these, when practiced with special breathing exercises, develops certain powers latent in the nerve centers and the different organs of the system. Another object in practicing *Asâna* is to remove the *Tamas* element which causes heaviness of the body, and to free the system from the effects of cold, catarrh, phlegm, rheumatism, and many other diseases. Some of the exercises increase the action of the stomach and liver, while others regulate the activities of the other organs. Tremor of the body and restlessness of the limbs, which are such frequent obstacles in the way of gaining control over the mind, may easily be removed by the practice of *Asâna*.

The reader may get an idea of the *Asâna* from the following descriptions:

I. Sit cross-legged on the floor, placing the left foot on the right thigh and the right foot on the left thigh, and keeping the body, neck, and head in a straight line.

II. After sitting in this posture, hold the right great toe with the right hand and the left great toe with the left hand (the hands coming from behind the back and crossing each other).

III. Sit straight on a level place, firmly inserting both insteps between the thighs and the calves of the legs.

IV. Assuming posture No. I, insert the hands between the thighs and the calves, and, planting the palms firmly on the ground, lift the body above the seat.

V. Sitting on the floor, stretch the legs straight in front, hold the great toes with the hands without bending the knees.

VI. Having accomplished this posture, touch the knees with the forehead. This *Asâna* rouses gastric fire, makes the loins lean, and removes many diseases.

VII. Holding the toes as in posture V, keep one arm extended and with the other draw the other toe towards your ear as you would do with the string of a bow.

VIII. Plant hands firmly on the ground, support the weight of the body upon the elbows, pressing them against the sides of the loins. Then raise the feet above the ground, keeping them stiff and straight on a level with the head.

This *Asâna,* according to Hatha Yoga, cures diseases of the stomach, spleen, and liver, and all disorders caused by an excess of wind, bile, or phlegm. It also increases the power of digestion.

IX. Lie upon the back on the floor at full length like a corpse, keeping the head on a level with the body. This *Asâna* removes fatigue and brings rest and calmness of mind.

The student of Hatha Yoga, having perfected himself in controlling some of these postures, should next take up the breathing exercises. He should carefully study the science of breathing in all its aspects. Posture No. I is one of the easiest and best *Asânas* for one who wishes to control the breath. It favors a tranquil circulation and slow respiration.

A beginner should first practice abdominal breathing through both nostrils, keeping a measured time for inspiration and expiration. Gradually he should be directed by his master to hold

23

the breath in and out. Practicing this internal and external suspension of breath for a few weeks, he should next take up alternate breathing. He may inspire through the left nostril for four seconds and expire through the right for four seconds, then reverse the order, breathing in through the right and out through the left. The alternate breathing exercises will purify the nerves and will make the student well-fitted for higher breathing exercises. The student should then breathe in through one nostril for four seconds, hold the breath counting sixteen seconds, and breathe out through the other nostril counting eight seconds. This exercise, if practiced regularly for three months, will generate new nerve-currents and develop the healing power that is latent in the system.

The Yogi who wishes to cure organic trouble or disease of any kind, should combine the higher breathing exercises with the different postures of the body which bear direct relation to the disturbed organ. He should arouse the healing power stored up at the base of the spine and direct it to the diseased part.

Hatha Yoga describes various methods for cleansing the internal organs. Some of them are extremely beneficial to those who suffer from chronic headache, or cold in the head, catarrh, dyspepsia, or insomnia.

The drinking of cold water through the nose removes headache or chronic cold in the head. A Hatha Yogi cleanses the passage between the nose and the mouth by passing soft cords of delicate thread through the nostrils and bringing them out at the mouth. He can pass the cord through one nostril and bring it out through the other. This purifies the head, makes the sight keen, and removes disease in the parts above the shoulders.

A Hatha Yogi cleanses the alimentary canal by swallowing a long piece of fine muslin three inches wide. He purges the impurities of the intestines by drawing water through the opening at the lower extremity of the alimentary canal. This he does with the help of breathing exercises without using any instrument. Then shaking

24

the water by the alternate exercise of the rectimuscles of the abdomen, he throws out the water through the same passage. An expert Yogi can wash the whole of the alimentary canal by drinking a large quantity of water and letting it pass through the opening at the lower extremity. Thus he becomes free from stomach or intestinal disorder. These exercises are especially recommended for those who are flabby, phlegmatic, or corpulent.

He cures insomnia by assuming posture No. IX, at the same time taking a few deep breaths and holding them after each inspiration.

A Hatha Yogi can swallow his tongue. It is said that he who can swallow his upturned tongue is freed from old age and death, conquers sleep, hunger and thirst, and rises above time. The powers of a perfect Hatha Yogi are indeed wonderful.

He can do and undo anything at his will. He is the master of all physical laws.

Thus we see that perfect health and longevity are the immediate results of the Hatha Yoga practices. To the real seeker after Absolute Truth, however, they have small value except as they become a means of attaining superconscious realization. According to him, if a man lives five hundred years and yet in that time does not reach the state of God-consciousness, he is little better than an oak tree which may outlast many generations and grow to great size, but is in the end only an oak tree. That man, on the contrary, who dies at the age of thirty, having realized his oneness with Divinity, has achieved infinitely more than he who possesses perfect health, longevity, psychic powers, or the gift of healing; for he has become a living God in this world and can point the way of salvation to all mankind. Therefore the exercises of Hatha Yoga should be practiced only so far as the earnest truth-seeker does not attain Râja Yoga, which alone will lead the soul to God-consciousness and perfect freedom.

Râja Yoga

HATHA YOGA, as we have already seen, is wholly devoted to the control of the functions of the body and to the mastery of the physical forces, its ideal being a sound constitution, well-fitted to overcome those physical and environmental conditions which stand as obstacles in the path of spiritual progress. Râja Yoga, on the contrary, deals entirely with the mind and psychic power and may be called the science of applied psychology. Its aim is to remove all mental obstructions and to gain a perfectly controlled, healthy mind. The main purpose of its training is to develop and strengthen the will as well as the power of concentration, and to lead the seeker after Truth through the path of concentration and meditation to the ultimate goal of all religion.

This path is called Râja Yoga or the Royal method (Râja means "king") because the power of concentration and will-power are not only greater than any physical force, but are essential to the acquisition of all other powers. The man who possesses a vigorous mind controlled by a well-developed will, with strong power of concentration, can easily become the master of physical nature and in a short time attain the realization of Truth; and it is the special province of Râja Yoga to teach how this can be accomplished. Its study has been encouraged by all those who have come in contact with the Râja Yogis of India either in ancient or modern times. It was extolled by Pythagoras, by Plato and the Neo-Platonists like Plotinus and Proclus, by the Gnostics and the Christian mystics of the middle ages; and even to-day it is in some measure practiced by some of the Roman Catholic monks and nuns of the higher orders. Spinoza, Kant, Schopenhauer, Ralph Waldo Emerson, spoke in praise of it, declaring its object to be the unravelling of the mystery of the nature of the human soul and the enfoldment of the latent powers existing in each individual. It has been proved by the living example of Yogis that through its practice that power can be acquired by which all other forces in the universe may be controlled; and Râja Yoga claims that whoever has gained mastery over his mind, can govern all the phenomena of nature.

It teaches that mind is the sovereign power of the universe, and that when its forces are properly concentrated upon any particular object, the true nature of that object will be revealed. Instead of using an instrument, if we properly utilize the mental powers which we already possess, and focus them absolutely upon one point, we can easily know all the particulars regarding the thing upon which they are directed. This object may be physical, mental, or spiritual. The concentrated mind of a Yogi may be compared to an electric search-light. By throwing the converged rays of his mind toward a distant object, whether gross or subtile, all the details of that object are illumined and made known to him. The vision of ordinary persons is not so penetrating because their mental forces are dissipated like the scattered rays of an ordinary light In the same way, if the mind can be concentrated upon internal objects or upon truths that exist in the realm of the universal, perfect knowledge of those things can be acquired.

Thus it becomes evident that the power, of concentration is greater than sense-power, or than that which can be gained by the help of instruments. If we can develop it by controlling our mental faculties, by making the mind introspective, and by checking all distractions which draw the mind outside; and can direct our concentrated mental energy toward our higher Self, the true nature of the individual ego will be revealed, and we shall realize that our immutable Self is the Soul of all, and that it is the same as the ultimate Reality of the universe. We shall then perceive that the Divine Being, whom in ignorance we worship as separate from ourselves, is not far from us, is not dwelling outside of us, but is our own omnipotent Self residing within us. We shall also recognize that the same Spirit is one and all-pervading, and that it is the Absolute Truth underlying the name and form of every phenomenal object. This knowledge will emancipate the soul from the bondage of ignorance.

Râja Yoga maintains that the outer world exists only in relation to the inner nature of each individual. What mind is to itself, the phenomenal world of sense-perception is to the mind. The external is only the reflection of the internal; that which we gain, that which we receive, is only the likeness or reflection of that which we have already given. Mental phenomena are merely the effects of invisible forces, which cannot be discovered by the senses or by any instrument which the human mind can invent. We may try forever to know these finer forces through the medium of our sense-perceptions, but we shall never arrive at any satisfactory result. A Râja Yogi understands this and therefore attaches little value to instruments.

He does not depend upon his sense-powers, but endeavors to gain all knowledge through the power of concentration. The science of Râja Yoga gives the various steps which lead to the attainment of this ideal. It explains clearly and scientifically the processes and methods by which concentration can be developed. It does not, however, ask the student to accept anything on hearsay, or to believe anything on the mere authority of scriptures or of writers. But it states certain facts, requests the student to experiment, experience the results, and draw his own conclusions.

There is nothing mysterious in the system of Râja Yoga. On the contrary, it points out the laws which govern so-called mysteries and explains under what conditions the phenomena of mysteries are produced. It shows that so long as the real cause of an event is unknown it appears mysterious to us. Standing upon the solid ground of logic and reason, the science of Râja Yoga unravels the riddles of the universe and directs the individual soul toward the attainment of the final end of all religions. Its principles are highly moral and uplifting. It helps the student to understand the true purpose of life and describes the way by which it may be fulfilled here and now. Râja Yoga tells us that we should not think so much of what will happen after death, but that we should make the best use of the present and unfold the latent powers which we already possess, while it reminds us again and again of the fact that the advancement made in this life will be the foundation of future progress. If we gain or develop certain powers before we die, those powers will not be lost, but will remain with us wherever we go after death; while external possessions, we know, cannot accompany us in the grave. The only things that we can carry out of life are our character, our experience and the knowledge gained therefrom. They are our real possessions; and it is these which Râja Yoga will help us to develop; since its chief object is to mould the character and lead the student to the knowledge of the divine nature of the soul. The methods which it teaches can be practiced without joining any secret organization, but merely by following the directions of a true Râja Yogi, who is pure and simple, whose mind is free from doubts, and who is unattached to the objects of the phenomenal plane.

The practice of Râja Yoga is divided into eight steps. The first four are the same as those of Hatha Yoga. The first and second, Yama and Niyama, include all the ethical laws that govern our moral nature. The strict observance of these laws is necessary to the practice of the other steps of Râja Yoga. All the fundamental principles of ethics expounded by Buddha and all the truths proclaimed in the Sermon on the Mount are contained in these first two steps. A beginner in the practice of Râja Yoga should live a strictly moral and pure life, otherwise he will not advance in this path, nor will he reach the highest Truth or realize the Divinity that dwells within him. A neophyte must remember that purity, chastity, and morality are the very cornerstones of the structure of the Science of Yoga. In the requirements of the first step we find non-killing, non-stealing, truthfulness, continence, forgivingness, firmness of character, kindness to all living creatures, simplicity, moderation in diet, and cleanliness. Non-killing must be in thought, word, and deed, so with truthfulness and non-stealing. The character must be firm, for the student must persist in the face of all obstacles until spiritual perfection is reached. He must not take up the study as a passing fad, only to satisfy his momentary curiosity, but must continue with patience and perseverance until the highest ideal is realized.

The second step includes austerities, forbearance, contentment, faith in the Supreme Being, charity, study, and self-surrender to the Divine will. All the physical exercises necessary for keeping the body in perfect condition are to be found in the third step.[1] Health is essential to the attainment of the highest knowledge. Those who are suffering from disease cannot make their mind steady, cannot fix their attention upon truths existing on the spiritual plane, because naturally their minds will be centered on the diseased parts of the body. A beginner, who possesses a healthy body and a well-balanced mind, should choose any *Asâna* or posture of the body in which he can sit firmly for a long time without feeling pain in the limbs. In the practice of Râja Yoga, however, one need not be so particular regarding the posture of the body. The student should simply observe that the spinal column is kept perfectly straight while practicing breathing lessons in a sitting posture.

Prânâyâma, or breathing exercises, constitute the fourth step. The practice of certain breathing exercises will remove many obstacles like dullness, laziness, and bodily weakness, and will be helpful in gaining control over the senses, sense organs, and nerve centers, as also in quieting the restlessness of the mind. Anyone who will practice such breathing exercises regularly, will acquire wonderful power over both his mind and his body. He who suffers from worry, anxiety, nervousness, or insomnia, can obtain excellent results even in a few days by the practice of proper breathing exercises. Those who have studied the science of breathing will know what these results are; but the main object of the Prânâyâma in Râja Yoga is to develop the power of concentration.

Making the mind introspective is the fifth step. It is called Pratyâhâra. If we can withdraw the mind from external objects, fix it on some inner object, and bring it under the control of the will, we shall accomplish all that is required in this step. Pratyâhâra is preparatory to concentration. Before the student is able to concentrate on any particular object he must learn to gather up his scattered mental powers. This process of collecting the powers of the mind and of restraining it from going out to external objects is what the Yogis designate as Pratyâhâra.

Concentration follows next. After going through the five preliminary steps, if one takes up concentration, the results achieved will be extraordinary. Those, however, who have not practiced the introductory steps will find this one extremely difficult, for the ground must be prepared before good results can be gained.

Meditation is the seventh stage, and through it one passes into Samâdhi or the state of superconsciousness, which is the eighth and last step. In this state the sixth sense of finer perception is developed, the spiritual eye is opened, and one comes face to face with the Divine Being dwelling within. In it the student realizes that his true Self is one with the universal Spirit, and he receives all the revelation and all the inspiration that can possibly come to the human soul. It may be thought by many that revelation proceeds from some external source, either through the favor of some angel or bright spirit or the extra-cosmic personal God, but a Yogi knows that revelation or inspiration is the disclosure of the higher Self within, and that the realization of spiritual truths comes to that soul which has reached the eighth step of Râja Yoga. Ceaseless effort, persistence, and perseverance in practice are necessary to attain to the state of superconsciousness. That which is realized in it cannot be revealed by

intellect or by any other mental faculty; therefore it is said that Truth cannot be attained by reading books or Scriptures, or by intellect or sense-perception, but by reaching the state of superconsciousness. Those who are longing to know the Truth, who are searching for the ultimate Reality of the universe, and are not satisfied with the knowledge gained through the senses or through the aid of instruments, should struggle hard to go into Samâdhi, because through it alone will they discover their ideal and reach the abode of happiness. Before, however, they can arrive at this state, they will have to follow faithfully the different steps already enumerated and with patience and perseverance overcome all the obstacles which beset the way.

There are many obstructions to Samâdhi, such as grief, disease, mental laziness, doubt, cessation of the struggle to attain Samâdhi, heaviness of body and mind, thirst for worldly things, false knowledge, non-attaining concentration, falling away from the state once attained, irregular breathing, etc. They can be easily avoided by regular practice under the guidance of a Yogi teacher. If a student try to practice by himself any of the exercises as given in Râja Yoga, 1 he may have some unpleasant experiences which may disturb his mind or nervous system; but if he have an experienced Râja Yogi to direct him, then he will have no difficulty in conquering all the obstacles and dangers, and in reaching the right destination. Some of the powers generated by these practices are too dangerous to be handled by an inexperienced student; they may not only injure him but may even drive him to insanity. There have, indeed, been many such cases among those who have tried to practice without the help of a well-qualified Guru or spiritual teacher.

Having removed all obstructions in this path, the student should be confident that he is approaching the final goal of Râja Yoga. When the superconscious realization is acquired all doubts will cease forever, all questions concerning the nature of the soul will be answered, the search after Truth will stop, the mind will become tranquil, and the soul will be emancipated from the bondage of ignorance and self-delusion. The Yogi will never again fall a victim to the attractions of the world or be distracted by objects of sense. The whole universe will appear to him as the play-ground of the Divine Being; and he will constantly feel that his body and mind are like instruments moving under the direction of the Almighty Will which is manifesting through all forms. Thus, having gained spiritual strength and illumination, he will become the conqueror of himself and the master of nature even in this life.

"He alone has reached happiness on this earth, he alone has conquered the world, who has gained perfect control over his mind and body, whose soul rests in tranquillity, and whose eyes behold Divinity in everything and everything in that Eternal Being, which is the Infinite Abode of existence, knowledge, and bliss absolute."

Karma Yoga

ONE of the significations of the word "Yoga" is "Dexterity in work." To render this meaning still more specific, the Sanskrit term "Karma," derived from the root verb "Kri," to act, is added. Taken in its literal sense, therefore, Karma signifies action, and refers to all actions whether of mind or body. Wherever there is activity of any kind, it is Karma. In this sense devotion, love, worship, meditation, concentration, discrimination are all Karma; as are also, for the same reason, eating, drinking, walking, talking, or performing any organic function.

Again, every action, as we are aware, is followed by reaction. No action can be separated from its result, as no cause can be absolutely disconnected from its effect. Consequently the secondary meaning of Karma embraces all reactions or results of actions. The chain of cause and sequence, known as the "law of causation," is also called Karma; and every action of body and mind is governed by the law of Karma or of action and reaction. Being subject to this natural law, we have been working in this world from the beginningless past, and reaping the results of our efforts, whether pleasant or unpleasant, good or evil.

When, furthermore, we consider that the effect of each action leaves its impression on the mind-substance, which impression becomes the seed of a fresh action of a similar nature, we understand the third meaning of the term. In this sense the word Karma includes the accumulated results of past actions or rather the seed forms of future activities.

Hence the character of an individual, which is the aggregate result of the works of his previous life may be called Karma. In the same way, the future life will be the sum-total of the results of the mental and physical actions of the present life.

Karma Yoga is, therefore, that branch of the Science of Yoga which discusses the three ideas conveyed by the word "Karma," explains the philosophy of work, describes the method by which the individual soul can extricate itself from the wheel of action and reaction, and having escaped from the irresistible law of causation by which every one is bound, can attain to perfect freedom, fulfill the highest purpose of life, and thus through right action alone reach the ultimate goal of all religion. It is the path best fitted for those who believe in no creed, who are not devotional, and who do not care to worship or pray to a personal God.

Karma Yoga teaches that the cause of the suffering, misery, disease, and misfortune, which overshadow our earthly life, lies in our own actions. We reap the fruit of that which we ourselves have sown. These causes are within us. We should blame neither our parents nor any evil spirit for our sufferings, but should look within ourselves to discover the source thereof. This branch of Yoga likewise describes the secret of work, by knowing which we can remove all causes of bondage and suffering, and enjoy freedom, peace, and happiness both here and after death. It tells us that every action inspired by the motive of desire for results attaches the soul to these results, and consequently becomes a source of bondage. The secret of work consists in working for work's sake and not for fruits. If this principle be applied to the actions of our daily lives, then every work done by us will help us to advance toward the perfect emancipation of the soul. Whoever performs his duties understanding the secret of work, becomes truly unselfish and eventually gains knowledge of his real Self, which is immortal and divine.

According to Karma Yoga, the true Self when it becomes identified with the limitations of the mind and the physical form, appears as "ego," "doer," or "actor," and performing work from various motives, remains attached to its results. We thus feel as one with our body and endeavor to enrich the narrow, limited self or "I" by getting something from that which is "not I." This imperfect knowledge of the "Self," or rather this ignorance of the true "Self," is the cause of selfishness.

From selfishness in turn proceeds all that desire for results which forces us to live and act like slaves. Karma Yoga shows us the way by which we can become conscious of our true Self, and, by widening the range of the limited "ego," can make it universal. When we have accomplished this, we shall live in the world working not from selfish motives, but for humanity, yet with as much interest in heart as we had when we worked for ourselves. Nor shall we then seek the comfort and pleasure of this little personality which is now the chief center of our interest and effort, but shall strive for the good of all.

Anyone who wishes to become a true Karma Yogi should clearly understand the philosophy of work, [1] and should remember that every action of body and mind must produce some effect which will eventually come back upon the doer; and that, if there be the smallest desire for result, it will be the seed of future action of a like nature. He should also realize that every action produces similar reaction. If the action be in harmony with the moral and physical laws which govern our lives, then the reaction which comes back upon the actor will bring only that which is good,-- peace, rest, fortune, health, and happiness. If, on the contrary, these laws are violated, then the result will be evil, producing restlessness, discomfort, loss of fortune, disease, and unhappiness.

A traveller in the path of Karma Yoga should not even think evil of another, because in the attempt to injure others we first injure ourselves. Every thought puts the mind-substance in a certain state of vibration and opens the door to the influence of such minds as are in the same state of vibration. Therefore when we cherish evil thoughts, we run the double risk of affecting other minds and of being influenced by all evil-minded persons holding

35

similar thoughts, nay, we expose our minds to all the evil thoughts that have been thought in the past and stored up in the mental atmosphere of the world. A corresponding result comes from the holding of good thoughts. This is the reason why evil-doers grow worse and worse every day, and the doers of good deeds become better and better.

A Karma Yogi should realize that there is one Being, or one Spirit, in the universe. Seeing this same Being or Spirit in all living creatures, he should recognize the rights of all and should not injure anyone either mentally or physically. Such a Yogi is truly unselfish; he is a blessing to the world and to humanity.

He who wishes to practice Karma Yoga should abandon attachment to the fruit of his labors, and learn to work for work's sake, keeping in mind the idea that by his work he is paying off the debt which he owes to parents, to society, to country, and to all mankind. Like a wet nurse he should take care of his children, realizing that they do not belong to him, but that they are placed in his charge in order that he and they may gain experience and unfold their latent powers and feelings.

A true Karma Yogi, furthermore, is he who recognizes that his real Self is not a doer of action, but that all mental and physical activity is merely the result of the forces of nature. Therefore he never claims that any work, whether good or bad, has been done by his true "Self." He lets his mind, intellect, and sense-organs work incessantly, while in his soul he holds steadfastly to the idea that he is the witness-like Knower of all activity, mental or physical. In this way he frees himself from the law of Karma and escapes from all the results of work which bind ordinary workers. Neither does he count success or failure in his daily life. He does his best in each effort put forth by him, and after performing his duty to the utmost of his ability, if he meets with failure he does not grieve, but, saying within himself that he did all that he could under the circumstances, he maintains his calmness and enjoys peace of mind even in the face of defeat.

The aim of a Karma Yogi is to live in the world and act like a master, not like a slave. Ordinary mortals implicitly obey the masters of desire and passion, following them without question or discrimination. But he who chooses the path of Karma Yoga seeks absolute control over desire and passion and directs the force manifesting through these channels toward the highest ideal of life--freedom of the soul.

In fulfilling all the duties of life the Karma Yogi takes refuge in love, making it the sole motive power behind every action of body and mind; and whenever he performs any duty, it is always through love. He understands that sense of duty is bondage, while work done through a feeling of love frees the soul and brings peace, rest, and, in the end, everlasting happiness.

All the great spiritual leaders of mankind, like Christ and Buddha, were Karma Yogis. They worked for humanity through love, and showed by their example how perfect freedom can be attained by right work. Buddha did not preach the worship of a personal God, but he established the truth that those who do not believe in a personal God and who are not devotional, can reach the highest goal of all religions by the path of Karma Yoga.

Bhakti Yoga

BHAKTI YOGA teaches that the final end of all religions can be reached through love and worship of the personal God, who is the Creator and Governor of the phenomenal universe. It leads to the same destination as all the other branches of Yoga, but is especially suited for such as are emotional in their nature and have the feeling of love and devotion highly developed. It is for those devotees who, conscious of their own weakness arising from lack of self-control and of knowledge, seek help from outside; and who, taking refuge in the Supreme, pray to Him for forgiveness and for pardon of sins committed through ignorance of the moral and spiritual laws that govern our lives.

All dualistic systems of religion, like Christianity, Judaism, and Mahometanism, which advocate the worship of a personal God, knowingly or unknowingly preach Bhakti Yoga and direct their adherents along this path.

The word "Bhakti" means devotion, while Yoga in this case signifies union of the individual soul with God. Hence Bhakti Yoga is the method of devotion by which true communion of the soul with the Supreme Deity is accomplished. It shows what kind of devotion and love for God will bring the soul into the most intimate relation with the Divine Being; and how even the ordinary feelings of a human heart, when directed Godward, can become the means of attaining spiritual oneness with the Soul of the universe. Râja Yoga tells us that desire, passion, love, hatred, pride, anger, must be completely conquered before perfection can be reached. A student of Râja Yoga must not only keep constant watch over his mind, but he must also faithfully practice the eight steps already described, if he would achieve his highest ideal; while in Bhakti Yoga we learn that all desires and passions, whether good or bad, can be directed towards God. Then, instead of binding the soul to worldliness and earthly attachment, they become a means of attaining God-consciousness and absolute freedom from selfishness and wickedness.

A follower of Bhakti Yoga should feel God as closely related to his soul as he possibly can; and regard Him not only as the Lord of the universe, but as father, mother, brother, sister, friend, or child. Even the relation existing between husband and wife may be cultivated and developed in the heart of a lover of God, intoxicated by the soul-stirring wine of Divine Love. When the whole heart and soul of a Bhakta or lover of God flow like the unbroken current of a mighty river, surmounting all barriers and dashing headlong toward the ocean of Divinity, he finds no other attraction in the world, holds no other thought, cherishes no other desire, speaks no other word, and sees no other thing than his most Beloved, the Omnipresent Deity. He resigns himself entirely to Him and surrenders his will to the will of the Almighty One. He works, but without thinking of results. Every action of his body and mind is performed simply to please his Beloved One. His motive power is love alone and by this he breaks asunder the chain of selfishness, transcends the law of Karma, and becomes free. Thus a true Bhakti Yogi, being constantly in tune with the Infinite, loses the sense of "I," "Me," and "Mine," and makes room for "Thou," "Thee," and "Thine."

A Bhakta never forgets his relation to his Beloved. His mind is concentrated and one-pointed; consequently meditation becomes easy for him. True devotion or continuous remembrance of the Divine Ideal leads to unceasing meditation, and ultimately lifts the soul into Samâdhi, where it realizes God and communes with Him undisturbed by any other thought, feeling, idea, or sensation. Becoming dead to sense phenomena, it lives on the spiritual plane of God-consciousness. Wherever such a Yogi casts his eyes, he sees the presence of the All-pervading Divinity and enjoys unbounded peace and happiness at every moment of his life. It is for this reason that Bhakti Yoga is considered to be the easiest of all methods. What a Râja Yogi attains only after years of practice, a Bhakta accomplishes in a short time through extreme devotion and love. That which a Karma Yogi finds so difficult to achieve, a Bhakti Yogi attains easily by offering the fruits of all his works to the Almighty Source of all activity and the ultimate end of all motives.

Bhakti Yoga has two grades,--the first is called "Gauni," or preparatory and includes all the preliminary practices; the second is "Para," or the state of supreme love and devotion to God. A beginner in Bhakti Yoga should first of all prepare the ground of his heart by freeing it from attachment to earthly objects and sense-pleasures; then by arousing in it extreme longing to see God, to realize Divinity, to go to the Source of all knowledge, and to reach perfection and God-consciousness in this life. He must be absolutely earnest and sincere. He should seek the company of a true lover of God, whose life is pure and spotless, who has renounced all worldly connections, and who has realized the true relation which the individual soul bears to the Universal Spirit. If, by good fortune, he meets such a real Bhakta, he should receive from him the seed of Bhakti, plant it in the ground of his heart, and by faithfully following the instructions of the master, take special care to keep it alive and make it grow, until it becomes a large tree bearing the fruit of Divine Love. He should have respect, reverence, and love for his master, who will open his spiritual eye and transmit his own spiritual powers to his soul. When these powers begin to work, the soul will be awakened from the deep sleep of ignorance and self-delusion.

The Guru, or spiritual eye-opener, knowing the natural tendency of the disciple, will advise him to look upon God as his Master, or as his Father or Mother, and will thus establish a definite relation between his soul and God. Henceforth the disciple should learn to worship or pray to the Supreme through this particular relation. At this stage symbols, rituals, ceremonies may appeal to his mind; or he may repeat some name of the Lord that signifies the special aspect of the Divinity corresponding to the relation which he bears to Him. Constant repetition of such a name will help the mind of the neophyte to become concentrated upon the Divine Being. During this period he should avoid such company, such places, and such amusements as make him forget his chosen Ideal. He should live a chaste and pure life, always discriminating right from wrong and struggling to control his passions and desires by directing them Godward. He should be angry with himself for not realizing his ideal; he should hate his sinful nature because it keeps him away from the path of Bhakti and prevents him from remembering his Beloved. Thus he will gradually succeed in correcting his faults and in gaining control over his animal nature.

A traveller on the path of Bhakti should observe cleanliness of body and mind, should be truthful, and lead a simple life, without injuring any living creature mentally or physically. He should not kill any animal for his food, neither should he covet that which does not belong to him. He should, furthermore, obey the laws of health which tend to make him physically strong, as well as those moral laws the violation of which weakens the mind.

So long as the devotee thinks of God with a form and believes that He is outside of his soul and of the universe, he can make a mental picture of Him and worship the Divine Ideal through that form; or he may keep before him some symbolic figure like the cross which will remind him of his Ideal at the time of devotion. But a Bhakta should never mistake the imaginary form or the symbolic figure for the real Ideal. Wherever there is such a mistake there is to be found spiritual degeneration and the expression of ignorance in the form of sectarianism, bigotry, fanaticism.

Gradually, as the Bhakta approaches God, he will rise above such dualistic conceptions and realize that his Beloved is not only transcendent but immanent in nature, that nature is His body, that He dwells everywhere, that He is the Soul of our souls and the Life of our life, that He is the one stupendous Whole while we are but His parts. The Bhakta then reaches that state which is called qualified non-dualism. He sees that from the minutest insect up to man all living creatures are related to the Iswara is a part is related to the whole. Therefore he cannot kill or injure any living being. Understanding that everything pertaining to any part belongs in reality to the whole, he says, "Whatever is mine is Thine"; and it is from this moment that absolute self-resignation and self-surrender to the will of the Iswara begin to reign supreme in the soul of the Yogi. Then he is able to say from the bottom of his heart, "Let Thy will be done," and never again can he forget that his soul is a part of the Iswara. His devotion henceforth consists in remembering this new relation, and his worship takes a new form. Whatever he does with mind or body becomes an act of worship of the Supreme Whole, for he realizes that he possesses no power that does not belong to God. Eating, drinking, walking, talking, and every other work of his daily life become acts of devotion, and the entire existence of such a Bhakta is a continuous series of acts of worship. Then the heart is purified and selfishness is dead.

The devotee thus rises to the second grade of Bhakti Yoga and begins to taste that Divine Love which is the fruit of the tree of Bhakti. Here all distinction between lover and Beloved disappears; the lover, the Beloved and Love all merge into one ocean of Divinity. The soul of the Bhakta is transformed, and manifesting omniscience, God-consciousness, perfect freedom, and all other Divine qualities, it attains to the highest ideal of Bhakti Yoga.

Jnâna Yoga

THE last is Jnâna Yoga, the path of wisdom. The word "Jnâna," being derived from the Sanskrit root Jnâ," to know, means knowledge; and the ideal which it holds up before its followers is the realization of that Absolute Truth, which is the one common source of all subjective and objective phenomena in the universe. It teaches that there is one life, one Being, one Reality, and that all notions of distinction and differentiation, that all beliefs in the permanent duality or multiplicity of existence are unreal and illusory.

Jnâna Yoga is based entirely upon the monistic principles of the *Advaita* or non-dualistic system of Vedânta. Its purpose is to show that subject and object are but the two expressions of one Absolute Being or Substance; that God and man, the Creator and the created, are only different aspects of one Universal Reality. Its aim is to resolve the divers phenomena into one ultimate Being, from which proceed all powers and all forces manifested in external and internal nature, and which is the abode of infinite intelligence and eternal happiness.

According to Jnâna Yoga, matter, mind, intellect, sense-powers, names, and forms are but the apparent manifestations of that one Substance which is called in Sanskrit Brahman. They may appear to us as real, but they have in truth only relative reality. The phenomena of the universe are like the waves in the ocean of Brahman. As waves rise in the sea, and after playing for a while, once more merge into it, so the waves of subject and object rise, live, and dissolve in the ocean of that Absolute Substance Brahman. Brahman is described in Vedânta as "That of which all animate and inanimate objects are born, by which they live, and into which they return after dissolution. It should be known and realized by all." It is the essence of Divinity. It is like the eternal canvas upon which the Creator or the Cosmic Ego and the created or individual egos are painted by Maya, the inscrutable creative power of the Infinite Being.

The chief object of Jnâna Yoga is to unify God and the individual Soul and to show the absolute oneness that exists between them on the highest spiritual plane. The individual ego; being the reflection or image of Divinity or Brahman, in its true nature is divine, and this true Self is known in Sanskrit as the *Âtman.* The knowledge of this oneness of the Âtman or subjective reality with Brahman, the Universal Truth, is described in Jnâna Yoga as the only means of attaining to complete liberation from the bondage of selfishness and from attachment to body and senses, which are the causes of all worldliness, unhappiness, and misery. The light of the knowledge of the Âtman and of its unity with Brahman alone will dispel the darkness of ignorance which prevents us from reaching the abode of Absolute Existence, Intelligence, and Bliss, and which now deludes us into identifying the individual Self with the body, senses, mind, and their modifications. This ignorance is designated in Sanskrit *Avidyâ* or ne-science, and is the source of all false knowledge, egotism, attachment to the lower self and to the world. Being deceived by the illusive power of *Avidyâ*, we mistake body for soul and soul for body, matter for spirit and spirit for matter. In ignorance of our true Self, we work solely to gratify selfish motives and to reap some result from our actions. But Jnâna Yoga would waken us from this sleep of ignorance, by showing us that the Âtman is immortal, unchangeable, all-knowing, and free by its own nature from eternity to eternity; that through the influence of *Avidyâ*, the individual ego thinks of itself as changeable and subject to birth and death, and forgetting that the fountain-head of freedom, knowledge, and everlasting happiness is abiding within, it seeks knowledge and happiness from outside and becomes the slave of desires and passions. It further reminds us that whatever we think or perform mentally or physically is like a dream in the sleep of self-delusion caused by the power of *Avidyâ*; that these dreams of the sleep of ignorance can be removed neither by work, nor by devotion, nor by meditation, but by the light and power of *Vidyâ*, the knowledge of the Âtman or Self and of its relation to Brahman.

This knowledge cannot be obtained as the result of any virtuous act or prayer, but comes to the soul when the intellect and heart have been purified by unselfish and righteous works, and when the individual ego begins to discriminate between the real and unchangeable Âtman and apparent and changeable matter or force. Jnâna Yoga teaches that right discrimination and proper analysis are indispensable to the acquisition of knowledge of the true Self and of the Reality which underlies phenomenal objects. It also declares that knowledge of the Self will bring to the soul the realization of Absolute Truth more quickly than the practice of Râja, Karma, or Bhakti Yoga.

The path of wisdom, therefore, is best fitted for those earnest and sincere seekers after Truth who have no leaning towards active life, who are not devotional in their nature, but who are preeminently intellectual, and who, having realized the transitory and ephemeral character of phenomenal objects, are no longer contented with sense-pleasures. It is for those who wish to be free from all fetters and attachments, and who care nothing for earthly prosperity, success, social honor, fame, or the fulfilment of personal ambitions; but whose sole desire is to know who they are in reality, what is their true nature, and what relation exists between their soul, God, and the universe.

A traveller along this path should be philosophical in tendency, should have a sharp intellect and a keen power of analyzing the true nature of things. He should also have a firm conviction that the ultimate Truth or Reality of the universe is unchangeable. Using the sword of right discrimination between the Self and the non-self, he should sever all ties, and should never allow himself to be overpowered by any external or internal influence. His mind should be undisturbed by passions or desires, his senses well controlled, and his body strong, healthy, and capable of bearing all hardships as well as of overcoming all environmental conditions. He should have dispassion; and be ever ready to renounce anything that does not help him in his realization of Truth. He must have absolute confidence in the teachings of Jnâna Yogins, or those who have become Seers of Truth by following the path of wisdom; and he must likewise have faith in the final Truths expounded by the monistic system of Vedânta.

The mind of a beginner in Jnâna Yoga must possess the power of perfect concentration and meditation; and his soul must be filled with the longing for absolute freedom from all relative conditions and from the laws which govern phenomena. He must realize that even the enjoyment of heavenly pleasures is a kind of bondage, since it keeps the soul entangled in the meshes of phenomenal relativity. Being well-armed with all these noble qualities as his weapons, a Jnâna Yogi should fight against phenomenal appearances, and with the ideal of the unity of the true Self and the Absolute Brahman ever before his mind's eye, he should march onward toward its realization, breaking down all names and forms with the hammer of right analysis, and cleaving all ties of attachment with the sword of proper discrimination. Nor should he stop until the goal is reached. He who goes through the path of wisdom, burns the vast forest of the trees of phenomenal names and forms by starting in it the fire of right knowledge. All these names and forms are produced by Maya, the inscrutable power of Brahman; and according to Jnâna Yoga this power of Maya is inseparable from Brahman as the power of heating is inseparable from fire. A Jnâna Yogi, in his search after Brahman, should reject all names and forms by saying "Not this," "Not this," until he realizes the one nameless, formless, and absolute Being of the universe, where the subject and the object, the knower, knowledge, and its object, losing their relativity, merge into the infinite Ocean of Blissful Existence and Supreme Intelligence.

A sincere seeker after Truth should hear over and over again that the Âtman or true Self is one with Brahman or the Eternal Truth; and should repeat such phrases as "I am Brahman," "I am one with the Absolute Source of knowledge, existence, and bliss." He should constantly think of the meaning of "*Tat Twain asi*"--"That thou art," and should devote his time to meditating upon this oneness until the light of Brahman illumines his soul, dispelling the darkness of *Avidyâ* and transforming his ego into the essence of Divinity.

Instead of worshipping a personal God like a Bhakta, a Jnâna Yogi should clearly understand the true significance of all His attributes as given in the different Scriptures--such as Creator or Governor of the universe, He is Spirit, infinite, omniscient, all-powerful, unchangeable, true, and one; and rejecting the worship of the personal God as an act proceeding from *Avidyâ* or ignorance of the divine nature of the Self or Âtman, he should seek that which is above all attributes and beyond all descriptions, which transcends the realm of thought and cannot be revealed by human intellect or understanding. He should realize that all conceptions of a personal God are more or less anthropomorphic, and that the Creator himself must be phenomenal since He can exist only in relation to the created object. A Jnâna Yogi, consequently, does not pray to the personal God or to any other Spirit or Being. To him prayers and devotions are useless and unnecessary. He does not seek any supernatural help or Divine mercy, for he is conscious of the omnipotent and omniscient nature of the Âtman, and knows that his true Self is beyond good and evil, above virtue and vice, unlimited by all laws, and that it reigns over nature in its own glory. He feels that it is the same in essence as the Creator or personal God. Instead of identifying himself with body, mind, senses, or intellect, he always remembers that he is the Âtman, which is birthless, deathless, sinless, fearless, immutable, eternally peaceful, and ever undisturbed by pleasant or unpleasant experiences, sensations, or mental and physical changes.

A true Jnâna Yogi constantly tries to keep himself above all phenomenal conditions, and incessantly repeats "I am Brahman," "Soham"--I am He, I am He. He says within himself:

"I am neither mind, nor intellect, nor ego, nor senses; I am neither earth, nor water, nor air, nor fire, nor ether, but my true nature is absolute existence, knowledge, and bliss. I am He, I am He."

"I am neither the organic activity nor am I the elements of the body, neither the sense of knowledge nor that of action, but I am absolute existence, knowledge, and bliss. I am He, I am He."

"I have neither hatred nor love, neither greed nor delusion, neither egotism nor pride nor vanity, neither creed nor faith, nor aim nor desire for freedom. I am absolute existence, knowledge, and bliss. I am He, I am He."

"I have neither virtue nor vice nor sin. neither pleasure nor pain, neither Scriptures nor rituals nor ceremonies. I am neither food nor am I the eater. I am absolute existence, knowledge, and bliss. I am He, I am He."

"I have neither death nor fear of death, nor birth nor caste distinction; neither father nor mother, neither friend nor foe, neither master nor disciple. I am absolute existence, knowledge, and bliss. I am He, I am He."

"I have neither doubt nor question. I am formless and all-pervading. I am the eternal Lord of nature and the master of the senses. I am neither bound nor free. I am one with Brahman. I am the omnipresent Divinity, I am the immutable Lord of all. I am absolute existence, knowledge, and bliss. I am He, I am He."

Thus constantly practicing discrimination and rising above all relativity and phenomenal appearances, a Jnâna Yogi realizes the Absolute, Unchangeable, Eternal Truth in this life and ultimately becomes one with it; because Jnâna Yoga declares that he who knows Brahman becomes Brahman, for the same reason that the knower of God can be no other than God himself. A Jnâna Yogi never forgets that his true Self is Brahman. Having attained to this supreme God-consciousness, he lives in the world like an eternal witness of all mental and physical changes. Ever happy and undisturbed, he travels from place to place, pointing out to mankind the way to absolute freedom and perfection. A perfect Jnâna Yogi, indeed, lives as the embodiment of the Absolute Divinity on this earth.

Science of Breathing

THE Science of Yoga with its various branches justly claims, as we have already seen, to unravel the mysteries of life and death. Some of the advanced thinkers in Western countries are beginning to understand the importance of this noble science and to explain the problems of existence by it; but modern physiologists, anatomists, biologists, and medical practitioners are still uncertain as to the proper solution of these problems; the more they investigate, the more doubts arise in their minds. Within the last fifty years the various researches in the different departments of science, such as physics, chemistry, physiology, and biology, have apparently ended in the conclusion that life is nothing but the result of physical and chemical actions in the organic structure, that there is no such thing as vital force distinct and separate from the physical and chemical forces which have been discovered in the scientist's laboratory.

Some of the students of science are even anxiously waiting in the vain expectation that some day they will hear of the discovery of a substance, artificially produced in the laboratory, which will live, move, grow, multiply, and die like a particle of living matter. The majority of modern thinkers, in fact, hold that vitality is merely the result of the mechanical activity of the organs; that life comes directly from dead matter, and obeys physical, chemical, and mechanical laws; that a living animal is nothing but a machine; and that all of his actions whether of body or mind are purely mechanical. They say that a living protoplasm is only a combination of certain chemical elements, subject to ordinary chemical laws; that living and non-living are one; and that the living comes directly from the non-living. According to these scientists a human being is no more than a mechanical resultant of certain chemical changes governed by the laws of physical nature. If, however, we ask them what force it is that determines these physical and mechanical modifications, what is the power that causes all these chemical changes in such numberless varieties, they answer that they do not know.

Are we really like machines, subject to mechanical laws and nothing more? Is our growth entirely due to the process of accretion and aggregation of matter in the non-living world? Are we merely some accidental precipitation, deposition, or crystallization of atoms and molecules which are governed by no power higher than the chemico-physical forces? Students of physiology now learn in their text-books this physico-chemical theory of the origin of life. They laugh at those who use such expressions as "vital energy," "vital force," "vitality," or "life force," in the sense of some power separate and distinct from the physico-chemical forces of nature. In fact, when they study physiology they throw aside all ideas of vitality or life force; they believe in a nature devoid of vitality or life, and try to explain the formation of brain cells, nerves, tissues, and the construction of the various organs of a living animal without recognizing the existence of a vital agency. A reaction, however, has taken place recently in Europe, and a class of scientific thinkers has appeared, Dr. Lionel S. Beale being the most prominent, who, having found no satisfactory explanation of life through these theories, have, after closer observation and experiment, come to the conclusion that there is a vital force entirely distinct from mechanical or physico-chemical forces, and which manifests itself through living particles of matter.

It is true that the human body is a machine, but not like any machine made by man. It is a self-moving, self-regulating, and self-adjusting, vital machine governed by will-power and intelligence. It was produced by a germ of life which possessed vitality, and which had the capability of becoming conscious, of willing, thinking, and producing psychic activity, in which are included all emotions and thoughts belonging to a human being. By a germ of life is meant that germ of matter or substance which contains the potentiality of life and mind. Although the manifestation of this vital force depends upon organic structure, still it is not the same as any of the familiar forces known to us; it is not like heat, electricity, magnetism, or molecular attraction. On the contrary, it is a force which governs and directs all these grosser physical forces. It is the director of the telegraphic current which notifies the energy of the muscle when and how to exert itself. It coordinates all automatic movements, controls the system as a whole as well as in detail, and is itself the principle of purely animal life. The special organ through which it functions chiefly, and which has been constructed to differentiate it from other energies, to give it a form and a purpose, and to afford it a vehicle of expression, is the spinal nerve of the vertebrateand the equivalent organ in other animals.

This mysterious and invisible vital energy or vital force is called in Sanskrit "Prâna." That branch of the Science of Yoga which treats of this mysterious force, describing its origin and nature, and teaching how it can be controlled and utilized to produce wonderful results, is known as the Science of Prâna. Ordinarily it is translated into English by the word "Breath," and called the "Science of Breath"; but Prâna is not simple breath. In the Upanishads it is defined as the cause of all motion and life in both the organic and inorganic worlds. Wherever there is the slightest expression of motion, life, or mind, from the smallest atom, or animalcule, or amœba, or bioplasm, up to the largest solar system and the highest man, it is the manifestation of the all-pervading force called Prâna. It is one, yet appears as manifold through its divers expressions. It is the mother of all forces, psychical, chemical, and physical. Vedânta Philosophy describes it as the ultimate generalization of the multiple forces of nature. It is indestructible; the death of the form through which it manifests cannot destroy it; but it must not be confounded with molecular attraction for it is much finer; it cannot be seen, touched, weighed, measured, or captured by any means.

According to Vedânta, before the beginning of creation the unconditioned causal state of the universe contained potential Prâna; Vedânta does not make the absurd statement that life has come from non-life. It does not admit that vital energy is the result of mechanical forces, but, on the contrary, tells us that it is a force, which operates simultaneously with physico-chemical forces. They are all, in fact, expressions of the one living energy of Prâna. Although some of the modern scientific monists acknowledge that all matter and force spring from a common source, or from one eternal energy, still at the same time they deny the existence of life or vitality in that energy and declare that it is not living. They try to prove that life is the product of some kind of motion of dead matter; while Vedânta teaches that all the phenomena of the universe have evolved out of the one eternal substance, which possesses Prâna or cosmic vital force, cosmic mind, cosmic intelligence, and consciousness. These may be interdependent, but as they all exist in a human being, so the infinite variety of forces exist in that one eternal living Being whose body is the universe.

The Science of Yoga claims that this Prâna is the final cause of all the manifested forces of nature. Why does an atom move and vibrate? A scientist does not know, but a Yogi says because of Prâna. That force which produces vibration in an atom or a molecule is one of the expressions of the energy of Prâna or the cosmic Life-principle. The same Prâna appears as that power by which a germ of life works on the physical plane, arouses motion in the molecules of its cells and builds up a suitable structure, repairs injuries and reproduces its kind. It causes activity in a protoplasm, in a bioplasm or an amœba, as well as in the highest man. It is closely related to the mind, which includes all the psychic activities and intelligence displayed by that germ in the different grades of its evolution. Vital power and mind are, indeed, two aspects of one Prâna. A germ of life possesses mentality as well as vitality, and the phenomena of these two aspects are most intimately connected with one another. In the science of Yoga the relation between mind and Prâna is described as that of a horse and a rider, Prâna being the horse which the individual mind rides. The body moves like an automobile carriage when it is propelled from within by the force of Prâna and guided by the driver of the intelligent mind. The activity of the mechanism of the body stops if Prâna or vital force ceases to vibrate. Again, when the vibration of Prâna is arrested, the mind no longer operates on the physical plane. It is for this reason that vital force or Prâna is called the medium through which the mind expresses its powers on the physical plane.

The animal organism is nothing but a mechanism for the manifestation of the powers of the soul. When the soul wishes to express certain powers on the material plane it creates through Prâna some suitable organism to fulfill its desire. If the mental activities of any living creature change, the organic structure of the nerves and cells will also change. Various experiments have been made by different scientists which clearly show that mental effort underlies all physiological conditions and organic functions. An abnormal activity of the mind will invariably give rise to certain pathological conditions, because it will affect the vital action; and when the vital power, which gives life to every cell of the body, is influenced, the cells will begin to vibrate in a different manner; and the result will be abnormal activity in the cells of the organs, which in turn will produce various diseases. Conversely, when the vital activity is normal, the psychic function is also natural. The mind is just as much affected by a diseased body as the physical system is disturbed by a diseased mind. He who can regulate his mentalities knows how to preserve his vitality and keep a healthy body; while he who has control over his vital functions understands the secret of keeping a healthy mind. The man who is thus able to dominate both body and mind is the master of himself, the king in his own conscious domain. But he who is not the master of himself lives like a slave to passion, to sense-objects, to wealth, property, ambition, and all earthly desires. Those who do not know how to regulate their vital forces are always unhappy, for they constantly suffer either mentally or physically.

Every irregular activity of the mind will produce chemical and physiological change in the nerve centers, in the organs, and eventually in the whole body. This can be shown by analyzing the chemical properties of the secretions of different organs, and especially by analyzing the breath. If we analyze the breath of a person who is strongly moved by anger or any other violent passion, we shall find that his whole system is poisoned for the time being. By letting his breath pass through a certain solution in a glass tube, we shall readily see that distinct changes are produced in the solution. These variations, furthermore, are only the outward signs of the internal modifications that have taken place in the entire nervous system. It is, in fact, these organic changes that modify the breath; but in a normal, healthy state of mind and body the chemical solution will remain perfectly unchanged. The breathing is then regular, deep, and strong. Every impulse of passion that takes possession of the mind, causes a corresponding variation in the respiratory functions; anger, hatred, or jealousy for instance, are marked by short, quick breath, while thoughts of peace, of true happiness, and of divine love produce long, deep breath.

There are various ways of learning the relation that exists between vital activity and mentality. A Yogi says that all abnormal and diseased conditions of the body are caused directly by imperfect or weak expression of the vital energy, and indirectly by improper mental activity. The curing of a disease, therefore, means the removing of the obstacles, which prevent the Prâna from working in an absolutely normal way. This can be done either by physical processes or by regulating the mental functions. A Yogi heals disease in himself by increasing the vital action; by rousing the latent powers of the Prâna, which is the source of all life force. He knows how to fill his whole body, nay, every cell, with increased vitality. By regulating the polarity of the cells through the higher vibrations of Prâna he generates a strong current of vibratory Prâna, directs its course through the disordered cells of his organs, and changes the structure of these cells by creating a rapid circulation of the blood charged with the healing power of Prâna, and sending it to the parts affected. In this way the cells are restored to their normal condition and the disease is cured. The Yogi does this consciously and in the most scientific manner with the help of breathing exercises accompanied by concentration. According to the Science of Yoga all nervous currents and all molecular motion in the brain cells and nerve centers are caused by this Prâna. If the molecules of the cells be filled with a new and strong current of Prâna or vital force, their vibration will be enormously increased; and this will enable them to throw off the impure matter that retarded their natural activity, and recover their normal healthy condition.

The same Prâna is also the propelling power in circulation. A Yogi says that the vital energy is stored up in the nerve centers of the spinal cord. It is the cause of the motion of the lungs, which in turn produces respiration; and respiration is the cause of the circulation of the blood and of all other organic activity. Modern physiology tells us that every portion of our body, every tissue and cell breathes; that the lung is nothing more than an instrument in the respiratory process, the chemical operation, which is the essential part of this function, occurring elsewhere in the cells and tissues themselves. The lung is only the door through which oxygen enters the system. The physiologists of the eighteenth century held quite different views; even the father of modern chemistry, Lavoisier himself (1743-1794), supposed that the main act of respiration took place in the lungs. What really happens is that oxygen, introduced into the lungs, filters through the thin walls of the pulmonary capillaries, where it finds in the red corpuscles of the blood a substance called hemoglobin, with which it unites to form a compound known as oxy-hemoglobin. And a very unstable compound it is, for throughout the tissues, in the capillary vessels of the whole body, oxygen is allowed to escape freely and to effect its work upon the cells. The blood, therefore, is merely a vehicle. The "organic combustions" do not occur in the lungs, their seat being in the cells and tissues throughout the whole system.

Physiological chemistry tells us that all things mineral, vegetable, and animal, are mainly composed of four principal elements-- oxygen, hydrogen, carbon, and nitrogen. Of these oxygen is of the greatest importance, since it is the most widely diffused, constituting by weight one-fifth of the atmosphere, eight-ninths of the ocean and all water, nearly one-half of solid rock and of every solid substance, and more than one-half of all vegetables and animals. If a man weighs one hundred and fifty pounds, one hundred and ten of his weight is oxygen. It is the chief cause of all activity in mechanical, chemical, muscular, and mental forces. The amount of energy or activity of an animal is determined by the amount of oxygen he respires; and the degree of force manifested in the human organism is in proportion to the rate at which oxygen is introduced into the system. It is the first requisite of vital action. Without it all other materials of life will be of little avail; and the respiratory organs are the medium through which it enters the system. The blood which has been once used in our bodies would be of no further service if it were not purified by the lungs. Ordinarily air when inhaled, contains 21 per cent oxygen, and when exhaled, 12 per cent, having lost 9 per cent. In a healthy adult man the average pulsation is 75 in a minute and about two ounces of blood are driven by each pulsation from the heart to the lungs, or nine pounds and six ounces in a minute. The quantity of blood in the human body is considered to be about one-fifth of the weight of the entire body, or twenty-eight pounds in a man weighing one hundred and forty pounds. The full quantity of blood in the system will, therefore, flow through the lungs in the short period of three minutes; in other words, the vast amount of thirteen thousand five hundred pounds in every twenty-four hours.

It is well known now that as a rule only one-sixth of the full capacity of the lungs is used; if the remaining five-sixths were properly brought into play who can say what marvellous results might not follow? Nature has not given capacity to any organ without a purpose; and we are sure that, if every one were to use the full capacity of his lungs, weak or diseased lungs would be a thing of the past. If we understand the science of breathing, we can develop our lung power to its utmost capacity; then by well-regulated breathing exercises we can purify every particle of matter in the cells of the organs, and with the help of the current of Prâna can ultimately drive out all physical weakness.

Faith-healers, mental-healers, and Christian Scientists cure disease without giving drugs; the Yogis of India do the same, but in a more scientific manner. Faith-healers and Christian Scientists ask us to believe in a certain thing and to declare that we are not suffering. A Yogi says that we can get better and surer results if through breathing exercises we can control the Prâna, increase the vital current, and fill the whole system with the healing power of Prâna. By polarizing the activity of the cells, and removing the obstacles that prevent the proper manifestation of the vital current in those cells, we shall get rid of the disease. If mental-healers and faith-healers knew the secret of controlling the Prâna, they would have been undoubtedly more successful in their attempts. Some among them are now beginning to take up breathing exercises, and perhaps in time they will learn the truths contained in the wonderful science of breathing.

Generally people who know nothing of this science think that it teaches merely the mechanical process of breathing in and out; but its province is much more extended, for it likewise shows how to control the Prâna, how to increase the vitality of the system by generating new nerve currents of a higher order, how to polarize the vibration of the cells, and how to awaken those powers which lie dormant on the sub-conscious plane as well as in the nerve centers of the spine. It also tells us that when the powers begin to manifest, we rise above the influences and changes to which ordinary mortals are subject. India is the only country where from ancient times this science of breathing has been carefully studied in all its aspects by the Yogis. Through centuries of investigation they discovered different methods of regulating the breath, following which marvellous results, both mental and physical, could be obtained. Out of these various discoveries grew up the science of breathing, which, besides the control of the breath, also explains what relation the process of respiration bears to Prâna, and how, by harmonizing the vibrations of nerve cells with the higher laws of life force, one gains mastery over Prâna. This control of Prâna brings complete subjugation of all the forces which govern the mind and body.

The aim of a Yogi is to establish absolute harmony between his vital actions and his mental functions, to transcend all laws, to rise above the influence of all environmental conditions, and to be the supreme ruler of the mind and of the entire system. According to the Yogi, this perfect self-mastery and consequent freedom do not come to one who has not learned the secret of regulating the vital energy, and who has not acquired the power to direct it wherever it is needed. Before anyone can control this invisible vital force, he must know its principal seat in the body; he must learn where this unseen king of physical activities is enthroned, who are his attendants, and how lie governs his kingdom.

A Yogi says that the king or Prâna resides with his attendants in the nerve centers of the spinal column. These centers are the main stations where this vital force is stored. There are many centers in the spinal cord out of which proceed the motor and sensory nerves which cover the whole body, including its organs. All sensations and motions of the limbs depend upon these nerve centers in the spinal column and the brain. There are two currents which flow in and out of the brain through the spinal column and nerves; they are called afferent and efferent currents--in Sanskrit, "Idâ" and "Pingalâ." They run through the anterior and posterior channels of the spinal cord, and these furnish the two paths over which the currents of Prâna travel. The nervous energy itself being scattered throughout the system, the only means of regulating it is by controlling the principal centers or stations in the spinal column. If, therefore, any one wishes to control the Prâna, he must first learn to govern the chief stations through which it works. After studying the relation of these different centers the Yogis found that there were six of primary importance. Those who wish to know their names can refer to the volume on "Râja Yoga" by the Swâmi Vivekananda.

According to the science of breath, the King of these six leading nerve centers in the spinal cord is enthroned in the center opposite the thorax; it is the respiratory center and in Sanskrit bears the name "Anâhata." It moves the lungs, causes respiration, and gives activity to all the other centers, which are dependent on it. If the royal center is disturbed or vibrates abnormally, those which are subject to it, and through them the whole system will act in a corresponding manner; and the result will be disease, organic trouble, or continued ill-health. So long, however, as the royal center is in a normal condition, the movement of the lungs which causes inspiration and expiration will be regular. Therefore the Yogi who desires to subjugate the nerve centers first strives to gain control over the respiratory center. The science of breathing teaches that, by regulating the breath, the motion of the lungs and the functions of the whole nervous system can be regulated. It also says that, by controlling the nerve centers in the spinal column, mastery over the currents flowing throughout the system, and ultimately over the mind itself, with its various dormant powers, can be easily gained. If the mental powers that are now latent on the subconscious plane can be aroused, all the experiences of past incarnations, and the impressions gathered during previous lives, will come up on the conscious plane and we shall remember them all.

The Yogis say that the great majority of people breathe irregularly and that there are differences in the breathings of men and women. The causes of this irregular breathing are many-- food, drink, fear, sickness, sorrow, nervous excitement, passion, anxiety. These do not affect the breath directly, but they do influence it indirectly by producing abnormal activity of Prâna, first in the nerve centers, then in the movement of the lungs, which expresses outwardly as irregular breathing. Hence irregularity of the breath is the external sign of abnormal action of the respiratory center in the spine.

A Yogi whose respiratory center functions regularly and is under perfect control is free from weakness, ill-health, and all disease. As, by controlling the activity of Prâna in the nerve centers, the movement of the lungs and the respiration are regulated, so, conversely, by regulating the breath, the lungs and nerve centers will be controlled, for they work simultaneously. Those who are suffering from ill-health should devote especial attention to the study of the science of breathing, as it is absolutely necessary to the building up of a healthy mind and a healthy body.

The chief aim of a Yogi is to observe his own nature closely and to learn clearly what forces are operating in his system, and what relation they bear to one another; for by gaining a complete knowledge of his own nature he will gain correct knowledge of the whole universe, since the laws that govern the human body are universal. All these laws are nothing but the modes in which Prâna operates in nature. Therefore a Yogi seeks first to understand the individual Prâna and the vital laws which govern his own system.

In India this fact was recognized and the science of breathing was carefully studied by the sages, who had no other ambition or purpose in life than to acquire knowledge for its own sake. They explained this science, practiced breathing exercises (noting the results), and instructed their pupils, but not to make a profession of it, or to earn money, or to gain fame in society. On the contrary, they refused to teach those who came to learn for professional ends; and it is because of this disinterestedness on their part that the knowledge of the Yogis is so pure and unadulterated by ambition or selfish motives. They also realized the dangers which might arise from ignorant practice of these exercises. Those who are studying under inexperienced teachers should be on their guard, for there is great risk in letting the nerve currents flow in a wrong direction. It may produce abnormal results and may even end in mental disorder. Right breathing, on the contrary, brings the greatest benefits to mankind when properly practiced; but if it is abused it must do a corresponding amount of harm, just as any medicine will when improperly applied. As by studying Materia Medica a man cannot cure himself without the aid of a trained physician, so the mere study of Yoga cannot bring about truly good results unless it is carried on under the guidance of an experienced Yogi. It should be remembered, furthermore, that in a written book everything is not given, that each constitution is different from every other, and that that which is helpful to one may not be so to another.

Anyone who practices faithfully, according to the instructions of an experienced living teacher, will surely gain highly beneficial results both in mind and body. He will learn how to manufacture vital force and to increase the vitality of his whole organism. He will be able to remove all impurities from his system and to overcome all abnormal and diseased conditions, that is, where decomposition and disorganization have not advanced too far. He will likewise no longer be a victim to cold, chills, Grip, fever, rheumatism, stiffness of the joints or muscles, paralysis, and other ills; for he knows how he can remove them by increasing the vibrations of Prâna and thus giving new life to the cells of the organs.

Every individual, whether old or young, man or woman, is bound to get some result if the breathing exercises be practiced faithfully for six months. By breathing exercises, however, is not meant here merely deep breathing, such as is taught by teachers of music, Delsarte, or physical culture. Deep breathing is very good for drawing a full supply or oxygen into the system, and undoubtedly has its value, especially for women who wear tight dresses. Many of the diseases from which they suffer are directly traceable to a lack of the adequate quantity of oxygen necessary for organic combustion and for the maintenance of the activity of the organs. The organs of many people in this country are undeveloped, or abnormally developed, because of the unnatural clothes worn; and for all such deep breathing will be exceedingly beneficial. But too much of it is injurious, as it inflates and strains the lungs, and, if continued, the increased development of the tissues will after a time decay and produce various troubles. Those who are taking lessons in deep breathing from inexperienced teachers should stop to consider this. By breathing exercises we mean that process by which control over the motion of the lungs and of the nerve centers, as also, in the end, over the Prâna or vital energy can be acquired.

A Yogi declares that the practice of breathing will bring whatever result is desired, whether physical, psychical, or spiritual. He who has gained perfect control over his breath can suspend it for hours, and through this generate a power in the system which will levitate the body, even counteracting the tremendous force of gravitation. A Yogi conquers death by the control of Prâna. There are many Yogis in India who can tell the exact moment when they will leave their bodies. They say, "I am going to depart on such a day at such an hour," and at the appointed time consciously give up their bodies in the presence of many. There are some again who can prolong life indefinitely, and can subsist for long periods without taking any kind of solid or liquid food.

When so much can be accomplished through the control of the vital energy of Prâna, it is not strange that these Masters say to the world:

"Oh, ye mortals, study the science of breathing; learn the secret of controlling Prâna or the vital energy; strive diligently to regulate the breath; for the control of Prâna will bring all happiness, earthly and spiritual, and through it will come perfect health, mastery of the body, and that Supreme Bliss which is eternal and everlasting.

Was Christ a Yogi?

IN considering whether or not Christ was a Yogi we should first understand how spiritual and how divine one must be before he can be called a Yogi. A true Yogi must be pure, chaste, spotless, self-sacrificing, and the absolute master of himself. Humility, unostentatiousness, forgiveness, uprightness, and firmness of purpose must adorn his character. A true Yogi's mind should not be attached to sense-objects or sense-pleasures. He should be free from egotism, pride, vanity, and earthly ambition. Seeing the ephemeral nature of the phenomenal world, and reflecting upon the misery, suffering, sorrow, and disease with which our earthly existence is beset, he should renounce his attachment to external things, which produce but fleeting sensations of pleasure, and should overcome all that clinging to worldly life which is so strong in ordinary mortals.

A true Yogi does not feel happy when he is in the company of worldly-minded people who live on the sense plane like animals. He is not bound by family ties. He does not claim that this is his wife and these are his children; but, on the contrary, having realized that each individual soul, being a child of Immortal Bliss, belongs to the Divine Family, he severs all family relations and worldly connections and thus becomes absolutely free. A true Yogi must always preserve his equanimity in the face of the unpleasant as well as of the pleasant experiences of life; and rising above good and evil he should remain undisturbed by the success or failure, the victory or defeat, which may come to him as the result of the actions of his body and mind.

A true Yogi, again, must have unswerving devotion to the Supreme Spirit, the Almighty and Omniscient Soul of our souls; and realizing that his body and mind are the playground of the omnipotent Cosmic will, be should resign his individual will to the universal, and should be ever ready to work for others, to live for others, and to die for others. All his works, so long as he is in the society of people, should be a free offering to the world for the good of humanity; but at other times he should resort to secluded places and live alone, constantly applying his mind to the highest spiritual wisdom that can be obtained in the state of superconsciousness, through meditation on the oneness of the individual soul with God, the Universal Spirit.

A true Yogi must see the same Divinity dwelling in all living creatures. He should also love all human beings equally. He should have neither friend nor foe in the ordinary sense of those terms. A true Yogi is illumined by the light of Divine Wisdom, therefore nothing remains unknown to him. Time and space cannot limit the knowledge and wisdom of a true Yogi. Past and future events will appear to him like things happening before his eyes. For him the light of divine wisdom has dispelled the darkness of ignorance, which prevents one from realizing the true nature of the soul, and which makes one selfish, wicked, and sinful. All psychic and spiritual powers serve him as their real master. Whatever he says is sure to come to pass. He never utters a word in vain. If he says to a distressed or suffering person, "Be thou whole," instantly that person will become whole.

The powers of a true Yogi are unlimited, there is nothing in the world that he cannot do. Indeed, he alone has free access to the storehouse of infinite powers; but he never draws therefrom any force merely to satisfy idle curiosity, or to gratify selfish motives, or to gain wealth and fame, or to get any return whatsoever. He does not seek worldly prosperity, and always remains unconcerned about the result of his works. Praise or censure does not disturb the peace of his mind. Angels or bright spirits and the spirits of ancestors rejoice in his company and adore him. A true Yogi is worshipped by all. Having neither home nor possessions of his own, he wanders from place to place, realizing that the canopy of heaven is the roof of his world-wide home. He is easily pleased by everybody irrespective of his caste, creed, or nationality, and with a loving heart he blesses those who rebuke or curse him. If his body be tortured or cut in pieces, he takes no revenge, but, on the contrary, prays for the welfare of his persecutor. Such is the character of a true Yogi.

From ancient times there have been many such true Yogis in India and other countries. The descriptions of their lives and deeds are furthermore as wonderful and as authentic as the life and acts of that illustrious Son of Man who preached in Galilee nearly two thousand years ago. The powers and works of this meek, gentle, and self-sacrificing Divine man, who is worshipped throughout Christendom as the ideal Incarnation of God and the Saviour of mankind, have proved that he was a perfect type of one who is called in India a true Yogi. Jesus the Christ has been recognized by his disciples and followers not only as an exceptionally unique character but as the only-begotten Son of God; and it is quite natural for those who know nothing about the lives and deeds of similar ideal characters of great Yogis and Incarnations of God who have flourished at different times both before and after the Christian era, to believe that no one ever reached such spiritual heights or attained to such realization of oneness with the Heavenly Father as did Jesus of Nazareth.

The greater portion of the life of Jesus is absolutely unknown to us; and as He did not leave behind Him any systematic teaching regarding the method by which one may attain to that state of God-consciousness which He Himself reached, there is no way of finding out what He did or practiced during the eighteen years that elapsed before His appearance in public. It is, therefore, extremely difficult to form a clear conception of what path He adopted. But we can imagine that, being born with unusually developed spiritual inclinations, He must have devoted his life and time to such practices as led Him to the realization of absolute Truth and to the attainment of divine consciousness, which ultimately gave Him a place among the greatest spiritual leaders of the world as well as among the disinterested Saviours of mankind.

India is the only country where not only a complete system of practices is to be found, but also a perfect method, by following which well-qualified aspirants can attain to Christhood or to that spiritual unfoldment and divine enlightenment which made Jesus of Nazareth stand before the world as the ideal type of spiritual perfection. By studying the lives, the acts, and the most systematic and scientific teachings of the great Yogis of India, and by faithfully following their example and precepts, an earnest disciple can, through the Yoga practices given in the various branches of the Vedânta philosophy, hope some day to become as perfect as the Son of Man. This assurance must be a comfort and a consolation to the soul that is struggling for the attainment of spiritual perfection in this life. One peculiarity, however, of the teachings of the great Yogis of India is that the acquirement of spiritual perfection is the goal for all, and that each individual soul is bound, sooner or later, to be perfect even as Christ was perfect. They claim that spiritual truths and spiritual laws are as universal as the truths and laws of the material world, and that the realization of these truths cannot be confined to any particular time, place, or personality. Consequently by studying the Science of Yoga anyone can easily understand the higher laws and principles, an application of which will explain the mysteries connected with the lives and deeds of saints, sages, or Incarnations of God, like Krishna, Buddha, or Christ.

A genuine seeker after Truth does not limit his study to one particular example, but looks for similar events in the lives of all the great ones, and does not draw any conclusion until he has discovered the universal law which governs them all. For instance, Jesus the Christ said, "I and my Father are one." Did He alone say it, or did many others who lived before and after Him and who knew nothing of His sayings, utter similar expressions? Krishna declared, "I am the Lord of the universe." Buddha said, "I am the Absolute Truth." A Mahometan Sufi says, "I am He"; while every true Yogi declares, "I am Brahman." So long as we do not understand the principle that underlies such sayings, they seem mysterious to us and we cannot grasp their real meaning; but when we have realized the true nature of the individual soul, and its relation to the universal Spirit, or God, or Father in Heaven, or the Absolute Truth, we have learned the principle and there is no further mystery about it. We are then sure that whosoever reaches this state of spiritual oneness or God-consciousness will express the same thought in a similar manner. Therefore if we wish to understand the character and miraculous deeds of Jesus of Nazareth, the surest way open to us is the study of the Science of Yoga and the practice of its methods.

This Science of Yoga, as has already been stated, explains all mysteries, reveals the causes of all miracles, and describes the laws which govern them. It helps us to unravel the secrets of nature and to discover the origin of such phenomena as are called miraculous. All miracles like "walking on the sea," "feeding a multitude with a small quantity of food," "raising the dead," which we read of in the life of Jesus, are described by the Yogis as manifestations of the powers that are acquired through long practice of Yoga. These powers are not supernatural; on the contrary, they are in nature, are governed by natural though higher laws, and are therefore universal. When these laws are understood, that which is ordinarily called miraculous by ignorant people, appears to be the natural result of finer forces working on a higher plane. There is no such thing as the absolutely supernatural. If a person's conception of nature be very limited, that which exists beyond that limit will seem to him supernatural, while to another, whose idea of nature is broader, the same thing will appear perfectly natural; therefore that miracle, or that particular act which is classed as a miracle by a Christian, can be explained by a Yogi as the result of higher or finer forces of nature. Why? Because his conception of nature is much wider than that of an ordinary man. We must not forget that nature is infinite, and that there are circles within circles, grades beyond grades, planes after planes, arranged in infinite succession; and the desire of a Yogi is to learn all the laws which govern these various planes, and to study every manifestation of force, whether fine or gross. His mind is not satisfied with the knowledge of one particular plane of existence; his aim is to comprehend the whole of nature.

Those who have read the gospel of Buddha, by Paul Carus, will remember that, five hundred years before the birth of Jesus the Christ, Shâriputra, Buddha's illustrious disciple, walked on the surface of the water across a mighty river named Shrâvasti. A similar account of crossing a wide river by walking on the water, we find in the life of Padmapâda, the disciple of Sankarâchârya, the best exponent of the Vedânta philosophy, who lived about 600 A.D. Krishna, the Hindu Christ, whose other name is Lord of the Yogis, raised the dead nearly fourteen hundred years before the advent of Christ. The transfiguration of Krishna is likewise most beautifully described in the tenth and eleventh chapters of the "Song Celestial," and, like Christ, he also fed a vast multitude of people with a small quantity of food. There are other instances of similar powers shown by great Yogis who came later; and these accounts are in every way as historical and as authentic as those of Jesus the Christ. Thus we see that all the miracles performed by Jesus are to be found as well in the lives of Hindu Yogis, who lived both before and after Him.

So long as an event is isolated it appears supernatural and miraculous; but if we see the same thing happening elsewhere under similar conditions, it assumes the aspect of a natural occurrence governed by natural law, and then comes a proper solution of the mystery as well as the rational explanation of that which was called a miracle. It is in this that the Science of Yoga renders especial service to the world, for more than any science it helps to reveal the secrets of nature and to explain the causes of all miraculous deeds.

A true Yogi goes to the source of all power and of all forces, studies the laws behind them, and learns the method of controlling them. He knows that the various forces of nature are but expressions of one universal, living, intelligent energy, which is called in Sanskrit "Prâna." He sees that all the forces of physical nature, like heat, gravitation, electricity, as also all mental forces such as mind, intellect, thought, are nothing but the manifestations of that one living self-existent force, "Prâna." This intelligent energy projects from its bosom innumerable suns, moons, stars, and planets into physical space. It has hurled this earth from the molten furnace of the sun, it has cooled it, bathed it in air and water, and clothed it with vegetable and animal life; it wings the atmosphere with clouds and spans the planes with rivers, it takes a fine minute substance and transforms it into something huge and gross; it moves the body, gives life and motion to every atom and molecule, and at the same time manifests itself as thought and intellect.

Why should it be impossible for one who has realized his oneness with this fountain-head of all power, who has learned the method of controlling all phenomena by comprehending the laws which govern them, and who has become the master of the world as was Jesus the Christ, to perform simple phenomena like walking on the sea, turning water into wine, or raising the dead? According to a true Yogi these acts of Jesus the Christ were only a few expressions of the Yoga powers which have been exercised over and over again by the Yogis in India. Thus we understand that Christ was one of these great Yogis born in a Semitic family.

Jesus was a great Yogi because He realized the transitory and ephemeral nature of the phenomenal world, and, discriminating the real from the unreal, renounced all desire for worldly pleasures and bodily comforts. Like a great Yogi He lived a life of seclusion, cutting off all connections with earthly friends and relatives, and having neither home nor possessions of His own.

Jesus the Christ was a great Karma Yogi, because He never worked for results; He had neither desire for name nor ambition for fame or for earthly prosperity. His works were a free offering to the world. He labored for others, devoted His whole life to help others, and in the end died for others. Being unattached to the fruits of His actions, He worked incessantly for the good of His fellow-men, directing them to the path of righteousness and spiritual realization through unselfish works. He understood the law of action and reaction, which is the fundamental principle of Karma Yoga, and it was for this reason that He declared, "Whatsoever a man soweth, that shall he also reap."

Jesus of Nazareth proved Himself to be a great Bhakti Yogi, a true lover of God, by His unswerving devotion and His whole-hearted love for the Heavenly Father. His unceasing prayers, incessant supplications, constant meditation, and unflinching self-resignation to the will of the Almighty made Him shine like a glorious morning-star in the horizon of love and devotion of a true Bhakti Yogi. Christ showed wonderful self-control and mastery over His mind throughout the trials and sufferings which were forced upon Him. His sorrow, agony, and self-surrender at the time of His death as well as before His crucifixion, are conclusive proofs that He was a human being with those divine qualities which adorn the soul of a true Bhakti Yogi. It is true that His soul labored for a while under the heavy burden of His trials and sufferings; it is also true that He felt that His pain was becoming wellnigh unbearable when He cried aloud three times, praying to the Lord, "O my Father, if it be possible, let this cup pass from me."

But He found neither peace nor consolation until He could absolutely resign His will to that of the Father and could say from the bottom of His heart, "Thy will be done." Complete self-surrender and absolute self-resignation are the principal virtues of Bhakti Yoga, and as Christ possessed these to perfection up to the last moment of His life, He was a true Bhakti Yogi.

Like the great Râja Yogis in India, Jesus knew the secret of separating His soul from His physical shell, and He showed this at the time of His death, while His body was suffering from extreme pain, by saying, "Father, forgive them, for they know not what they do." It is quite an unusual event to see one imploring forgiveness for his persecutors while dying on the cross, but from a Yogi's point of view it is both possible and natural. Râmakrishna, the greatest Yogi of the nineteenth century, whose life and sayings have been written by Max Müller, was once asked, "How could Jesus pray for His persecutors when He was in agony on the cross?" Râmakrishna answered by an illustration: "When the shell of an ordinary green cocoanut is pierced through, the nail enters the kernel of the nut too. But in the case of the dry nut the kernel becomes separate from the shell, and so when the shell is pierced, the kernel is not touched. Jesus was like the dry nut, i.e., His inner soul was separate from His physical shell, and consequently the sufferings of the body did not affect him." Therefore He could pray for the forgiveness of His persecutors even when His body was suffering; and all true Yogis are able to do the same. There have been many instances of Yogis whose bodies have been cut into pieces, but their souls never for a moment lost that peace and equanimity which enabled Jesus to forgive and bless His persecutors. By this Christ proved that, like other Yogis, His soul was completely emancipated from the

69

bondage of the body and of the feelings. Therefore Christ was a Yogi.

Through the path of devotion and love Jesus attained to the realization of the oneness of the individual soul with the Father or the Universal Spirit, which is the ideal of a Jnâna Yogi as well as the ultimate goal of all religions. A Jnâna Yogi says: "I am He"; "I am Brahman"; "I am the Absolute Truth"; "I am one with the Supreme Deity." By good works, by devotion, love, concentration, contemplation, long fasting, and prayer, Jesus the Christ realized that His soul was one with God, therefore He may be said to have attained the ideal of Jnâna Yoga.

Like Krishna, Buddha, and all other great Yogis of India, Jesus healed the sick, opened the eyes of the blind, made the lame walk, and read the secret thoughts of His disciples. He knew exactly what Judas and Peter were going to do; but there was nothing supernatural in any of His actions, there was nothing that cannot be done again over and over by a true Yogi, and there was nothing in His life that cannot be explained rationally by the Science of Yoga and the Philosophy of Vedânta. Without the help of this science and this philosophy Jesus the Christ cannot be fully understood and appreciated. By studying His character, on the other hand, in the light of the Vedânta Philosophy we shall be able not only to understand Him better, but to have a larger appreciation of His true glory.

Material science now scoffs at His miracles, but they are corroborated by the Science of Yoga and confirmed by the deeds of the great Yogis of India. No devout Christian need for a moment fear that physical science can ever undermine the work of Jesus so long as the Science of Yoga is there to sustain all that He did. Let him study the character of Jesus through the Philosophy of Vedânta and I am sure that he will understand Him better and be a truer Christian, a more genuine disciple of the Son of Man than ever before. Let him follow the teachings of Yoga and he will some day become perfect like Christ.

It is through the teachings of Vedânta that the Hindus have learned how to glorify the character of Jesus; so also it is through Vedânta that a Christian will learn to adore the great Yogis like Krishna, Buddha, Râmakrishna, and others. It is through Vedânta that a Christian will be able to see how Divinity dwells in all animate and inanimate objects, and thus comprehending the true relation of the individual soul to the Supreme Spirit, will be enabled to say with the great Yogi Jesus the Christ, "I and my Father are one," and reach salvation in this life.

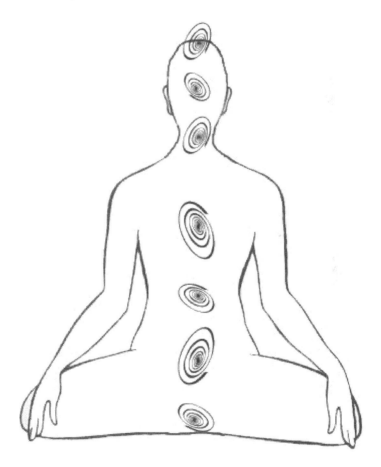

www.chakrahealingsounds.com

VEDANTA PHILOSOPHY
FIVE LECTURES
ON REINCARNATION
BY
SWAMI ABHEDANANDA
Edited by Dr.Jane Ma'ati Smith

CONTENTS

www.chakrahealingsounds.com
www.subliminalselfhypnosis.com

REINCARNATION

The visible phenomena of the universe are bound by the universal law of cause and effect. The effect is visible or perceptible, while the cause is invisible or imperceptible. The falling of an apple from a tree is the effect of a certain invisible force called gravitation. Although the force cannot be perceived by the senses, its expression is visible. All perceptible phenomena are but the various expressions of different forces, which act as invisible agents upon the subtle and imperceptible forms of matter. These invisible agents or forces together with the imperceptible particles of matter make up the subtle states of the phenomenal universe.

When a subtle force becomes objectified, it appears as a gross object. Therefore, we can say, that every gross form is an expression of some subtle force acting upon the subtle particles of matter. The minute particles of hydrogen and oxygen when combined by chemical force, appear in the gross form of water. Water can never be separated from hydrogen and oxygen, which are its subtle component parts. Its existence depends upon that of its component parts, or in other words, upon its subtle form. If the subtle state changes the gross manifestation will also change. The peculiarity in the gross form of a plant depends upon the peculiar nature of its subtle form, the seed. The peculiar nature of the gross forms in the animal kingdom depends upon the subtle forms, which manifest variously in each of the intermediate stages between the microscopic unit of living matter and the highest man. The gross human body is closely related to its subtle body. Not only this, but every movement or change in the physical form is caused by the activity and change of the subtle body. If the subtle body be affected or changed a little, the gross body will also be affected similarly. The material body being the expression of the subtle body, its birth, growth, decay and death depend upon the changes of the subtle body. As long as the subtle body remains, it will continue to express itself in a corresponding gross form.

Now let us understand clearly what we mean by a subtle body. It is nothing but a minute germ of a living substance. It contains the invisible particles of matter, which are held together by vital force, and it also possesses mind or thought-force in a potential state, just as the seed of a plant contains in it the life force and the power of growth.

According to Vedanta, the subtle body consists of "Antahkaranam", that is, the internal organ, or the mind substance, with its various modifications, mind, intellect, egoism, memory, the five instruments of perception: the powers of seeing, hearing, smelling, tasting and touching; the five instruments of action, such as the powers of seizing, moving, speaking, evacuating, and generating, and the five Pranas. Prana is a Sanskrit word which means vital energy or the life-sustaining power in us.

Although Prana is one, it takes five different names on account of the five different functions it performs. This word Prana includes the five manifestations of the vital force: First, that power which moves the lungs and draws the atmospheric air from outside into the system. This is also called Prana. Second, that power which throws out of the system such things as are not wanted. It is called in Sanskrit Apana. Third, it takes the name of Samana, as performing digestive functions and carrying the extract of food to every part of the body. It is called Udana when it is the cause of bringing down food from the mouth through the alimentary canal to the stomach, and also when it is the cause of the power of speech. The fifth power of Prana is that which works in every part of the nervous system from head to foot, through every canal, which keeps the shape of the body, preserves it from putrefaction, and gives health and life to every cell and organ. These are the various manifestations of the vital force or Prana. These subtle powers together with the non-composite elements of the gross body, or the ethereal particles of subtle matter, and also with the potentialities of all the impressions, ideas and tendencies which each individual gathers in one life, make up his subtle body. As a resultant of all the different actions of mind and body, which an individual performs in his present life, will be the tendencies and desires in his future life; nothing will be lost.

Every action of body or mind. which we do, every thought which we think, becomes fine, and is stored up in the form of a Samskara, or impression in our minds. It remains latent for some time, and then it rises up in the form of a mental wave and produces new desires. These desires are called in Vedanta, Vasanas. Vasanas, or strong desires, are the manufacturers of new bodies. If Vasana, or longing for worldly pleasures and objects remains in anybody, even after hundreds of births, that person will be born again. Nothing can prevent the course of strong desires. Desires must be fulfilled sooner or later.

Every voluntary or involuntary action of the body, sense or mind must correspond to the dormant impressions stored up in the subtle body. Although growth, the process of nourishment and all the changes of the gross physical body take place according to the necessarily acting causes, yet the whole series of actions, and consequently every individual act, the condition of the body which accomplishes it, nay, the whole process in and through which the body exists, are nothing but the outward expressions of the latent impressions stored up in the subtle body. Upon these rests the perfect suitableness of the animal or human body to the animal or human nature of one's impressions. The organs of the senses must therefore completely correspond to the principal desires, which are the strongest and most ready to manifest. They are the visible expressions of these desires. If there be no hunger or desire to eat, teeth, throat and bowels will be of no use. If there be no desire for grasping and moving, hands and legs will be useless. Similarly it can be shown that the desire for seeing, hearing, etc., has produced the eye, ear, etc. If I have no desire to use my hand, and if I do not use it at all, within a few months it will wither away and die. In India there are some religious fanatics who hold up their arms and do not use them at all; after a few months their arms wither and become stiff and dead. A person who lies on his back for six months loses the power of walking. There are many such instances, which prove the injurious effects of the disuse of our limbs and organs.

As the human form, generally, corresponds to the human will, generally, so the individual bodily structure corresponds to the character, desires, will and thought of the individual. Therefore the outer nature is nothing but the expression of the inner nature. This inner nature of each individual is what re-incarnates or expresses itself successively in various forms, one after another. When a man dies the individual ego or Jiva (as it is called in Sanskrit), which means the germ of life or the living soul of man, is not destroyed, but it continues to exist in an invisible form. It remains like a permanent thread, stringing together the separate lives by the law of cause and effect. The subtle body is like a water-globule, which sprang in the beginningless past from the eternal ocean of Reality; and it contains the reflection of the unchangeable light of Intelligence. As a water-globule remains sometimes in an invisible vapory state in a cloud, then in rain or snow or ice, and again as steam or in mud, but is never destroyed, so the subtle body sometimes remains unmanifested and sometimes expresses itself in gross forms of animal or human beings, according to the desires and tendencies that are ready to manifest. It may go to heaven, that is, to some other planet, or it may be born again on this earth. It depends on the nature and strength of one's life-long tendency and bent of mind. This idea is clearly expressed in Vedanta. "The thought, will or desire which is extremely strong during lifetime, will become predominant at the time of death and will mould the inner nature of the dying person. The newly moulded inner nature will express in a new form." (Bhagavad Gita.)

The thought, will or desire which moulds the inner nature has the power of selecting or attracting such conditions or environments as will help it in its way of manifestation. This process corresponds in some respects to the law of "natural selection." We shall be better able to understand that process by studying how the seeds of different trees select from the common environments different materials, and absorb and assimilate different quantities of elements. Suppose two seeds, one of an oak and the other of a chestnut, are planted in a pot. The power of growth in both the seeds is of the same nature. The environments, earth, water, heat and light are the same. But still there is some peculiarity in each of the seeds, which will absorb from the common environments different quantities of elements and other properties which are fit to help the growth of the peculiar nature and form of the fruit, flower, leaves of each tree. Suppose the chestnut is a horse-chestnut. If, under different conditions, the peculiar nature of the horse-chestnut changes into that of a sweet chestnut, then, along with the changes in the seed, the whole nature of the tree, leaves, fruits will also be changed. It will no more attract, absorb or assimilate those substances and qualities of the environments which it did when it was a horse-chestnut. Similarly, through the law of "natural selection" the newly moulded thought-body of the dying person will choose and attract such parts from the common environments as are helpful to its proper expression or manifestation. Parents are nothing but the principal parts of the environment of the re-incarnating individual. The newly moulded inner nature or subtle body of the individual will by the law of "natural selection" involuntarily choose, or be unconsciously drawn to, as it were, its suitable parents and will be born of them. As, for instance, if I have a strong desire to become an artist, and if after a life-long struggle I do not succeed in being the greatest, after the death of the body I will be born of such parents and with such environments as will help me to become the best artist.

The whole process is expressed in Eastern philosophy by the doctrine of the Reincarnation of the individual soul. Although this doctrine is commonly rejected in the West, it is unreservedly accepted by the vast majority of mankind of the present day, as it was in past centuries. The scientific explanation of this theory we find nowhere except in the writings of the Hindus; still we know that from very ancient times it was believed by the philosophers, sages and prophets of different countries. The ancient civilization of Egypt was built upon a crude form of the doctrine of Reincarnation. Herodotus says: "The Egyptians propounded the theory that the human soul is imperishable, and that where the body of any one dies it enters into some other creature that may be ready to receive it." Pythagoras and his disciples spread it through Greece and Italy. Pythagoras says: "All has soul; all is soul wandering in the organic world, and obeying eternal will or law."

In Dryden's Ovid we read:

"Death has no power the immortal soul to slay,
That, when its present body turns to clay,
Seeks a fresh home, and with unlessened might
Inspires another frame with life and light."

It was the keynote of Plato's philosophy. Plato says: "Soul is older than body. Souls are continually born over again into this life." The idea of Reincarnation was spread widely in Greece and Italy by Pythagoras, Empedocles, Plato, Virgil and Ovid. It was known to the Neo-Platonists, Plotinus and Proclus. Plotinus says: "The soul leaving the body becomes that power which it has most developed. Let us fly then from here below and rise to the intellectual world, that we may not fall into a purely sensible life by allowing ourselves to follow sensible images...." It was the fundamental principle of the religion of the Persian Magi. Alexander the Great accepted this idea after coming in contact with the Hindu philosophers. Julius Caesar found that the Gauls had some belief regarding the pre-existence of the human soul. The Druids of old Gaul believed that the souls of men transmigrate into those bodies whose habits and characters they most resemble. Celts and Britons were impressed with this idea. It was a favorite theme of the Arab philosophers and many Mahomedan Sufis. The Jews adopted it after the Babylonian captivity. Philo of Alexandria, who was a contemporary of Christ, preached amongst the Hebrews the Platonic idea of the pre-existence and rebirth of human souls. Philo says: "The company of disembodied souls is distributed in various orders. The law of some of them is to enter mortal bodies, and after certain prescribed periods be again set free." John the Baptist was according to the Jews a second Elijah; Jesus was believed by many to be the re-appearance of some other prophet. (See Matt, xvi, 14, also xvii, 12.) Solomon says in his Book of Wisdom: "I was a child of good nature and a good soul came to me, or rather because I was good I came into an undefiled body."

The Talmud and Cabala teach the same thing. In the Talmud it is said that Abel's soul passed into the body of Seth, and then into that of Moses. Along with the spread of the Cabala this doctrine (which was known as Transmigration and Metempsychosis) "began to take root in Judaism and then it gained believers even among men who were little inclined towards Mysticism. Juda ben Asher (Asheri) for instance, discussing this doctrine in a letter to his father endeavored to place it upon a philosophical basis." (Jewish Encyclopedia, Vol. XII, p. 232.) We also read, "The Cabalists eagerly adopted the doctrine on account of the vast field it offered to mystic speculations. Moreover it was almost a necessary corollary of their psychological system. The absolute condition of the soul is, according to them, its return, after developing all those perfections, the germs of which are eternally implanted in it, to the Infinite Source from which it emanated. Another term of life must therefore be vouchsafed to those souls which have not fulfilled their destiny here below, and have not been sufficiently purified for the state of union with the Primordial Cause. Hence if the soul, on its first assumption of a human body and sojourn on earth, fails to acquire that experience for which it descended from heaven and becomes contaminated by that which is polluting, it must reinhabit a body till it is able to ascend in a purified state through repeated trials." This is the theory of the Zohar, which says: "All souls are subject to transmigration; and men do not know the ways of the Holy One, blessed be He! They do not know that they are brought before the tribunal both before they enter into this world and after they leave it; they are ignorant of the many transmigrations and secret probations which they have to undergo, and of the number of souls and spirits which enter into this world and which do not return to the palace of the Heavenly King. Men do not know how the souls revolve like a stone which is thrown from a sling. But the time is at hand when these mysteries will be disclosed."

Like many of the Church Fathers the Cabalists used as their main argument in favor of the doctrine of metempsychosis the justice of God. But for the belief in metempsychosis, they maintained, the question why God often permits the wicked to lead a happy life while many righteous are miserable would be unanswerable. Then too the infliction of pain upon children would be an act of cruelty unless it is imposed in punishment of sin committed by the soul in a previous state. Isaac Abravanel sees in the commandment of the Levirate a proof of the doctrine of metempsychosis for which he gives the following reasons: (1) God in His mercy willed that another trial should be given to the soul, which having yielded to the sanguine temperament of the body had committed a capital sin, such as murder, adultery, etc.; (2) it is only just that when a man dies young a chance should be given to his soul to execute in another body the good deeds which it had not time to perform in the first body; (3) the soul of the wicked sometimes passes into another body in order to receive its deserved punishment here below instead of in the other world where it would be much more severe.

Christianity is not exempt from this idea. Origen and other Church Fathers believed in it. Origen says: "For God, justly disposing of his creatures according to their desert, united the diversities of minds in one congruous world, that he might, as it were, adorn his mansion (in which ought to be not only vases of gold and silver, but of wood also and clay, and some to honor and some to dishonor) with these diverse vases, minds or souls. To these causes the world owes its diversity, while Divine Providence disposes each according to his tendency, mind and disposition." He also says: "I think this is a question how it happens that the human mind is influenced now by the good, now by the evil. The causes of this I suspect to be more ancient than this corporeal birth." The idea of Reincarnation spread so fast amongst the early Christians that Justinian was obliged to suppress it by passing a law in the Council of Constantinople in 538 A.D. The law was this: "Whoever shall support the mythical presentation of the pre-existence of the soul, and the consequently wonderful opinion of its return, let him be Anathema." The Gnostics and Manichaeans propagated the tenets of Reincarnation amongst the mediaeval sects such as the Bogomiles and Paulicians. Some of the followers of this so-called erroneous belief were cruelly persecuted in 385 A.D. In the seventeenth century some of the Cambridge Platonists, as Dr. Henry More and others, accepted the idea of rebirth. Most of the German philosophers of the middle ages and of recent days have advocated and upheld this doctrine. Many quotations can be given from the writings of great thinkers, like Kant, Scotus, Schelling, Fichte, Leibnitz, Schopenhauer, Giardano Bruno, Goethe, Lessing, Herder and a host of others. The great skeptic Hume says in his posthumous essay on "The Immortality of the Soul," "The metempsychosis is therefore the only system of this kind that philosophy can hearken to." Scientists like Flammarion and Huxley have supported this doctrine of Reincarnation. Professor Huxley says: "None but hasty thinkers will reject it on the ground of inherent absurdity. Like the doctrine of evolution itself, that of transmigration has its roots in the world of reality."

Some of the theological leaders have preached it. The eminent German theologian Dr. Julius Muller supports this theory in his work on "The Christian Doctrine of Sin." Prominent theologians, such as Dr. Dorner, Ernesti, Ruckert, Edward Beecher, Henry Ward Beecher, Phillips Brooks, preached many a time touching the question of the pre-existence and rebirth of the individual soul. Swedenborg and Emerson maintained it. Emerson says in his essay on Experience, "We wake and find ourselves on a stair. There are stairs below us which we seem to have ascended; there are stairs above us, many a one, which go upward and out of sight."

Almost all of the poets, ancient or modern, profess it. William Wordsworth says in "Intimations of Immortality:"

"The soul that rises with us, our life's star,
Hath had elsewhere its setting,
And cometh from afar."

Tennyson writes in the "Two Voices;"

"Or, if through lower lives I came--
Tho' all experience past became,
Consolidate in mind and frame--
I might forget my weaker lot;
For is not our first year forgot?
The haunts of memory echo not."

Walt Whitman says in "Leaves of Grass:"

"As to you, Life, I reckon you are the leavings of many deaths,
No doubt I have died myself ten thousand times before."

Similar passages can be quoted from almost all the poets of different countries. Even amongst the aboriginal tribes of Africa, Asia, North and South America, traces of this belief in the rebirth of souls is to be found. Nearly three-fourths of the population of Asia believe in the doctrine of Reincarnation, and through it they find a satisfactory explanation of the problem of life. There is no religion which denies the continuity of the individual soul after death. Those who do not believe in Reincarnation try to explain the world of inequalities and diversities either by the one-birth theory or by the theory of hereditary transmission. Neither of these theories, however, is sufficient to explain the inequalities that we meet with in our everyday life. Those who believe in the one-birth theory, that we have come here for the first and last time, do not understand that the acquirement of wisdom and experience is the purpose of human life; nor can they explain why children who die young should come into existence and pass away without getting the opportunity to learn anything or what purpose is served by their coming thus for a few days, remaining in utter ignorance and then passing away without gaining anything whatever. The Christian dogma, based on the one-birth theory, tells us that the child which dies soon after its birth is sure to be saved and will enjoy eternal life and everlasting happiness in heaven. The Christians who really believe in this dogma ought to pray to their heavenly Father for the death of their children immediately after their birth and ought to thank the merciful Father when the grave closes over their little forms. Thus the one-birth theory of Christian theology does not remove any difficulty. Two great religions, Judaism with its two offspring- Christianity and Mahomedanism- and Zoroastrianism, still uphold the one-birth theory.

The followers of these, shutting their eyes to the absurdity and unreasonableness of such a theory, believe that human souls are created out of nothing at the time of the birth of their bodies and that they continue to exist throughout eternity either to suffer or to enjoy because of the deeds performed during the short period of their earthly existence. Here the question arises why should a man be held responsible throughout eternity for the works, which he was forced or predestined to perform by the will of the Lord of the universe? The theory of predestination and grace, instead of explaining the difficulty, makes God partial and unjust. If the omnipotent personal God created human souls out of nothing, could He not make all souls equally good and happy? Why does He make one to enjoy all the blessings of life and another to suffer all miseries throughout eternity? Why is one born with good tendencies and another with evil ones? Why is one man virtuous throughout his life and another bestial? Why is one born intelligent and another idiotic? If God out of His own will made all these inequalities, or, in other words, if God created one man to suffer and another to enjoy, then how partial and unjust must He be! He must be worse than a tyrant. How can we worship Him, how call Him just and merciful?

Some people try to save God from this charge of partiality and injustice by saying that all good things of this universe are the work of God, and all evil things are the work of a demon or Satan. God created everything good, but it was Satan who brought evil into this world and made everything bad. Now let us see how far such a statement is logically correct. Good and evil are two relative terms; the existence of one depends upon that of the other. Good cannot exist without evil, and evil cannot exist without being related to good. When God created what we call good, He must have created evil at the same time, otherwise He could not create good alone. If the creator of evil, call him by whatever name you like, had brought evil into this world, he must have created it simultaneously with God; otherwise it would have been impossible for God to create good, which can exist only

85

as related to evil. As such they will have to admit that the Creators of good and evil sat together at the same time to create this world, which is a mixture of good and evil. Consequently, both of them are equally powerful, and limited by each other. Therefore neither of them is infinite in powers or omnipotent. So we cannot say that the Almighty God of the universe created good alone and not the evil.

Another argument which the Vedantists advance in support of the theory of Reincarnation, is that "Nothing is destroyed in the universe." Destruction in the sense of the annihilation of a thing is unknown to the Vedantic philosophers, just as it is unknown to the modern scientists. They say "non-existence can never become existence and existence can never become non-existence;" or, in other words, that which did not exist can never exist, and conversely that which exists in any form can never become non-existent. This is the law of nature. As such, the impressions or ideas which we now have, together with the powers which we possess, will not be destroyed but will remain with us in some form or other. Our bodies may change, but the powers, Karma, Samskaras or impressions and the materials which manufactured our bodies must remain in us in an unmanifested form. They will never be destroyed. Again science tells us that that which remains in an unmanifested or potential state must at some time or other be manifested in a kinetic or actual form. Therefore we shall get other bodies, sooner or later. It is for this reason said in the "Bhagavad Gita": "Birth must be followed by death and death must be followed by birth." Such a continuously recurring series of births and deaths each germ of life must go through. Another consideration is that the beginning, ending and continuing are conceptions of the human mind; their significance depends entirely upon our conception of time. But we all know that time has no absolute existence. It is merely a form of our knowledge of our own existence in relation to that of nature. The conception of time vanishes at the sleep of death, just as it does every night when we are in sound sleep. Death resembles the state of our sound sleep. The soul wakes up from the sleep of death just in the same manner as the insects awake in spring after sleeping the long and rigid winter-sleep, as a chrysalis in the bed of a cocoon spun by itself in autumn. Nature teaches us the great lesson of rebirth and the similarity between sleep and death by the rejuvenation of the chrysalis in the spring. After death the soul wakes up and puts on or manufactures the garment of a new body, just in the same manner as we put on new clothes after throwing away the old and worn-out ones. Thus the soul continues to manifest itself over and over again either on the human or any other plane of existence, being bound by the Law of Karma or of Cause and Sequence.

"Death, so called, is but older matter dressed
In some new form. And in a varied vest,
From tenement to tenement though tossed,
The soul is still the same, the figure only lost."

Poem on Pythagoras, Dryden's Ovid.

Here it may be asked, if we existed before our birth why do we not remember? This is one of the strongest objections often raised against the belief in pre-existence. Some people deny the existence of the soul in the past simply because they cannot remember the events of their past. Others, again, who hold memory as the standard of existence, say, if our memory of the present ceases to exist at the time of death, with it we shall also cease to be; we cannot be immortal; because they hold that memory is the standard of life, and if we do not remember then we are not the same beings. Vedanta answers these questions by saying that it is possible for us to remember our previous existences. Those who have read "Raja Yoga" will recall that in the 18th aphorism of the third chapter it is said: "By perceiving the Samskaras one acquires the knowledge of past lives." Here the Samskaras mean the impressions of the past experience which lie dormant in our subliminal self, and are never lost. Memory is nothing but the awakening and rising of latent impressions above the threshold of consciousness. A Raja Yogi, through powerful concentration upon these dormant impressions of the subconscious mind, can remember all the events of his past lives. There have been many instances in India of Yogis who could know not only their own past lives but correctly tell those of others. It is said that Buddha remembered five hundred of his previous births.

Our subliminal self, or the subconscious mind, is the storehouse of all the impressions that we gather through our experiences during our lifetime. They are stored up, pigeon-holed there, in the Chitta, as it is called in Vedanta. "Chitta" means the same subconscious mind or subliminal self which is the storehouse of all impressions and experiences. And these impressions remain latent until favorable conditions rouse them and bring them out on the plane of consciousness. Here let us take an illustration: In a dark room pictures are thrown on a screen by lantern-slides. The room is absolutely dark. We are looking at the pictures. Suppose we open a window and allow the rays of the midday sun to fall upon the screen. Would we be able to see those pictures? No. Why? Because the more powerful flood of light will subdue the light of the lantern and the pictures. But although they are invisible to our eyes we cannot deny their existence on the screen. Similarly, the pictures of the events of our previous lives upon the screen of the subliminal self may be invisible to us at present, but they exist there. Why are they invisible to us now? Because the more powerful light of sense-consciousness has subdued them. If we close the windows and doors of our senses from outside contact and darken the inner chamber of our self, then by focusing the light of consciousness and concentrating the mental rays we shall be able to know and remember our past lives, and all the events and experiences thereof. Those who wish therefore to develop their memory and remember their past should practice Raja Yoga and learn the method of acquiring the power of concentration by shutting the doors and windows of their senses. And that power of concentration must be helped by the power of self-control. That is, by controlling the doors and windows of our own senses.

These dormant impressions, whether we remember them or not, are the chief factors in moulding our individual characters with which we are born, and they are the causes of the inequalities and diversities which we find around us. When we study the characters and powers of geniuses and prodigies we cannot deny the pre-existence of the soul. Whatever the soul has mastered in a previous life manifests in the present. The memory of particular events is not so important. If we possess the wisdom and knowledge which we gathered in our previous lives, then it matters very little whether or not we remember the particular events, or the struggles which we went through in order to gain that knowledge. Those particular things may not come to us in our memory, but we have not lost the wisdom. Now, study your own present life and you will see that in this life you have gained some experience. The particular events and the struggles which you went through are passing out of your memory, but the experience, the knowledge which you have gained through that experience, has moulded your character, has shaped you in a different manner. You will not have to go through those different events again to remember; how you acquired that experience is not necessary; the wisdom gained is quite enough.

Then, again, we find among ourselves persons who are born with some wonderful powers. Take, for instance, the power of self-control. One is born with the power of self-control highly developed, and that self-control may not be acquired by another after years of hard struggle. Why is there this difference? Bhagavan Sri Ramakrishna was born with God-consciousness, and he went into the highest state of Samadhi when he was four years old; but this state is very difficult for other Yogis to acquire. There was a Yogi who came to see Ramakrishna. He was an old man and possessed wonderful powers, and he said: "I have struggled for forty years to acquire that state which is natural with you." There are many such instances which show that pre-existence is a fact, and that these latent or dormant impressions of previous lives are the chief factors in moulding the individual character without depending upon the memory of the past. Because we cannot remember our past, because of the loss of memory of the particular events, the soul's progress is not arrested. The soul will continue to progress further and further, even though the memory may be weak.

Each individual soul possesses this storehouse of previous experiences in the background, in the subconscious mind. Take the instance of two lovers. What is love? It is the attraction between two souls. This love does not die with the death of the body. True love survives death and continues to grow, to become stronger and stronger. Eventually it brings the two souls together and makes them one. The theory of pre-existence alone can explain why two souls at first sight know each other and become attached to each other by the tie of friendship. This mutual love will continue to grow and will become stronger, and in the end will bring these lovers together, no matter where they go. Therefore, Vedanta does not say that the death of the body will end the attraction or the attachment of two souls; but as the souls are immortal so their relation will continue forever.

The Yogis know how to develop memory and how to read past lives. They say, time and space exist in relation to our present mental condition; if we can rise above this plane, our higher mind sees the past and future just as we see things before our eyes. Those who wish to satisfy the idle curiosity of their minds may spend their energy by trying to recollect their past lives. But I think it will be much more helpful to us if we devote our time and energy in moulding our future and in trying to be better than we are now, because the recollection of our former condition would only force us to make a bad use of the present. How unhappy he must be who knows that the wicked deeds of his past life will surely react on him and will bring distress, misery, unhappiness or suffering within a few days or a few months. Such a man would be so restless and unhappy that he would not be able to do any work properly; he would constantly think in what form misery would appear to him. He would not be able to eat or even sleep. He would be most miserable. Therefore we ought to regard it as a great blessing that we do not recollect our past lives and past deeds. Vedanta says, do not waste your valuable time in thinking of your past lives, do not look backward during the tiresome journey through the different stages of evolution, always look forward and try first to attain to the highest point of spiritual development; then if you want to know your past lives you will recollect them all. Nothing will remain unknown to you, the Knower of the universe. When the all-knowing Divine Self will manifest through you, time and space will vanish and past and future will be changed into the eternal present. Then you will say as Sri Krishna said to Arjuna, in the "Bhagavad Gita:" "Both you and I have passed through many lives; you do not recollect any, but I know them all."

HEREDITY AND REINCARNATION

Those who accept the theory of heredity deny the existence of the human soul as an entity separable from the gross physical organism. Consequently they do not discuss the question whether the individual soul existed in the past or will continue to exist after the death of the body. This kind of question does not disturb their minds. They generally maintain that the individual soul is inseparable from the body or the brain or nervous system; consequently what we call soul or the conscious entity or the thinker is produced along with the birth of the organism or brain, lasts as long as the body lasts and dies when the organism is dissolved into its elements. But those, on the other hand, who accept the theory of Reincarnation admit the existence of soul as a conscious entity which is independent of the physical organism, that it continues to live after death and that it existed before the birth of the body. The theory of heredity has always been supported by the materialistic scientists, atheists and agnostics of all ages and also by those who believe in the special creation of the first man and woman at a certain definite time and that their qualities, character, life and soul have been transmitted to all humanity through successive generations. The commonly accepted meaning of the theory of heredity is that all the well-marked peculiarities, both physical and mental, in the parents are handed on to the children; or, in other words, heredity is that property of an organism by which its peculiar nature is transmitted to its descendants.

In the whole history of humanity there has never been a time when this question of heredity has been discussed so minutely and in so many different ways as it has been in the present century. Although this theory was known in the East by the ancient Vedanta philosophers, by the Buddhists of the pre-Christian era and by the Greek philosophers in the West, still it has received a new impetus and has grown with new strength since the introduction of the Darwinian theory of the evolution of species. Along with the latest discoveries in physiology, biology, embryology and other branches of modern science,the popular simple meaning of heredity--that the offspring not only resemble their parents among animals as well as among men, but inherit all the individual peculiarities, life and character of their parents- has taken the shape of the most complicated and difficult problem which it is almost impossible to solve. Our minds are no longer satisfied with Haeckel's definition that heredity is simply an overgrowth of the individual, a simple continuity of growth; but we want to know the particular method by which hereditary transmission takes place. We ask, how can a single cell reproduce the whole body of the offspring, its mind, character and all the peculiarities of an organism? Out of the myriads of cells of which a body is composed, what kind of cell is that which possesses the power of reproducing the peculiarities, both mental and physical, which are to be found in the form of the new-born babe? This is the most puzzling of all the problems which the scientific mind has ever encountered. The fundamental question connected with the theory of heredity is: How can a single cell of the body contain within itself all the hereditary tendencies of the hypothesis of the continuity of the germ-plasm gives an identical starting-point to each successive generation, and thus explains how it is that an identical product arises from all of them. In other words, the hypothesis explains heredity as part of the underlying problems of assimilation and of the causes which act directly during ontogeny.

According to Weismann, all the peculiarities which we find in an organism are not inherited by the organism from that of the parents, but he says: "Nothing can arise in an organism unless the predisposition to it is pre-existent, for every acquired character is simply the reaction of the organism upon a certain stimulus." Therefore the germ-cells do not inherit all the peculiarities of the parents, but possess the predisposition or a potentiality of the tendencies which gradually develop into individual characters.

We will be able to understand his theory better from the following quotations, which give his own words. He says: "I have called this substance 'germ-plasm,' and have assumed that it possesses a highly complex structure, conferring upon it the power of developing into a complex organism." Again he says: "There is, therefore, continuity of the germ-plasm from one generation to another. One might represent the germ-plasm by the metaphor of a long, creeping rootstock from which plants arise at intervals, these latter representing the individuals of successive generations. Hence it follows that the transmission of acquired characters is an impossibility, for if the germ-plasm is not formed anew in each individual, but is derived from that which preceded it, its structure, and, above all, its molecular constitution, cannot depend upon the individual in which it happens to occur, but such an individual only forms, as it were, the nutritive soil at the expense of which the germ-plasm grows, while the latter possessed its characteristic structure from the beginning, viz., before the commencement of growth. But the tendencies of heredity, of which the germ-plasm is the bearer, depend upon this very molecular structure, and hence only those characters can be transmitted through successive generations which have been previously inherited, viz., those characters which were potentially contained in the structure of the germ-plasm. It also follows that those other characters which have been acquired by the influence of special external conditions, during the lifetime of the parent, cannot be transmitted at all." In conclusion, Weismann writes: "But at all events we have gained this much, that the only facts which appear to directly prove a transmission of acquired characters have been refuted, and that the only firm foundation on which this hypothesis has been hitherto based has been destroyed."

Thus we see how far the theory of heredity has been pushed by the great scientific investigators of the present age. We have no longer any right to believe in the old oft-refuted hypothesis which assumes that each individual organism produces germ-cells afresh again and again and transmits all its powers developed and acquired by the parents; but, on the contrary, we have come to know to-day that parents are nothing but mere channels through which these germ-plasms or germ-cells manifest their peculiar tendencies and powers which existed in them from the very beginning. The main point is that the germs are not created by the parents, but that they existed in previous generations.

Now, what are those germs like? Wherefrom do they acquire these tendencies, these peculiarities? That is another very difficult problem. Dr. Weismann and his followers say that these peculiarities are gained or inherited "from the common stock," but what that common stock is they do not explain. Where is that common stock and why will certain germs acquire certain tendencies and other germs retain other peculiarities? What regulates them? These questions are not solved. So far we have gathered from Dr. Weismann's explanation that the parents are not the creators of the germs but, on the contrary, that the germs existed before the birth of the body, before the growth of the body, in previous generations, or in the common stock of the universe. The previous generations are dead and gone, so we may say that they existed in the universe. We cannot now believe the old, crude, often-refuted idea that God creates the germ at the time of birth and puts into it all the powers and peculiarities of the parents. This theory makes God unjust and partial, so it does not appeal to us any more. We need better and more rational explanations. The one-birth theory, which has been preached by Christian ministers and other religionists for so many years, does not remove the difficulties, does not explain the cause of the inequalities and diversities, does not answer the question whether we acquire all the tendencies and peculiarities of the parents or whether acquired characters cannot be transmitted. We have already seen that these questions are left unsolved by the one-birth theory of Christianity and of Judaism. But this theory of "continuity of the germ-plasm" pushes the question of heredity to the door of Reincarnation. If modern science can explain what that common stock is and why and how these germs retain those peculiarities and tendencies, then the answer will be complete and not until then. The Vedanta philosophy, however, has already explained the cause of the potentiality in the germ of life or "germ-plasm" or germ-cell.

Vedanta solves this difficulty by saying that each of these germ-plasms or germ-cells is nothing but the subtle form of a reincarnating individual, containing potentially all the experiences, characters, tendencies, and desires which one had in one's previous life. It existed before the birth of the body and it will continue after the death of the body. This germ or subtle body is not the same as the astral body of the Theosophists, or the double of the metaphysical thinkers or the disembodied spirit of the Spiritualists; but it is an ethereal center of activity-physical, mental and organic. It is a center which possesses the tendency to manifest these powers on different planes of existence. It contains the minute particles of matter or ethereal substance and the life principle or vital energy by which we live and move. It also possesses the mental powers and sense powers; but all these remain latent, just as in a seed we see that the powers of growth, of assimilation and of producing flowers and fruits are latent.

At the time of death the individual soul contracts and remains in the form of a germ of life. It is for this reason, Vedanta teaches, that it is neither the will of God nor the fault of the parents that forms the characters of children, but each child is responsible for its tendencies, capacities, powers and character. It is its own "Karma" or past actions that make a child a murderer or a saint, virtuous or sinful. The stored-up potentialities in a subtle body manifest in the character of an individual.

The argument advanced by the supporters of the theory of hereditary transmission does not furnish a satisfactory explanation of the cause of the inequalities and diversities of the universe. Why is it that the children of the same parents show a marked dissimilarity to their parents and to each other?

Why do twins develop into dissimilar characters and possess opposite qualities, although they are born of the same parents at the same time and brought up under similar conditions and environments? How can heredity explain such cases? Suppose a man has five children; one is honest and saintly, another is an idiot, the third becomes a murderer, the fourth a genius or prodigy, and the fifth a cripple and diseased. Who made these dissimilarities? They cannot be accidents. There is no such thing as an accident. Every event of the universe is bound by the law of cause and effect. There must be some cause of these inequalities. Who made one honest and saintly, another an idiot, and so forth? Parents? That cannot be. They never dreamed that they would beget a murderer or a villain or an idiot. On the contrary, all parents wish their children to be the best and happiest. But in spite of such desires they get such children. Why? What is the cause? Does the theory of heredity explain it? No, not at all. Suppose a man, twenty-four years old, who has certain traits, like musical or artistic talents, such as painting and so on, has a crooked nose and other peculiarities, like cross-eyes, which resemble those of his grandfather. Suppose his grandfather died six years before he was born. Now, those who believe in the theory of heredity will say that this young man inherited all these peculiarities from his grandfather. When did he inherit? His grandfather had died six years before he was born. He inherited, of course, in the form of that germ. What is that germ like? A minute protoplasm, a jelly-like substance, and if you examine it with a powerful microscope you will hardly find any difference between it and the proto-plasmic germ of a dog, or of a cat, or of a tree. It is smaller than a pin's head. And in that state this young man inherited all these peculiarities from his grandfather; or, in other words, before he had a nose, he got a crooked nose; before he had eyes, he inherited cross-eyes, and before he had any brain, he inherited all the wonderful powers-his musical and artistic talents. Does it not seem absurd to you? Even if we admit this theory of heredity, then what do we understand? That the whole of this young man existed in the form of a protoplasm before he was born. His cross-eyes, his crooked nose, his artistic talents—all these pre-existed in the form of a protoplasmic cell. This leads up to the same thing which is taught by the theory of Reincarnation, or, in other words, if it be possible for this young man to remain in the form of a protoplasm and inherit all these things before his birth, why cannot we believe that the soul or the subtle body of this young man possessed them from the very beginning? According to Vedanta this young man was not the creature of his grandfather, but he had his own independent existence; only by coming through the channel of his parents he had received certain characteristic impressions, just as a tree in its process of growth will receive from the environments certain peculiarities when it assimilates those properties.

The doctrine of Reincarnation alone can explain satisfactorily and rationally the diversities among children and the reason of the many instances of uncommon powers and genius displayed in childhood. The theory of heredity has up to this time failed to give any good reason for them. Why is it that Pascal, when twelve years old, succeeded in discovering for himself the greater part of plane geometry. How could the shepherd Mangiamelo, when five years old, calculate like an arithmetical machine. Think of the child Zerah Colburn: when he was under eight years of age he could solve the most tremendous mathematical problems instantly and without using any figures. "In one instance he took the number 8 and raised it up progressively to the sixteenth power and instantly mentioned the result which contained 15 figures--281,474,976,710,656." Of course he was right in every figure. When asked the square root of numbers consisting of six figures, he would state the result instantly with perfect accuracy. He used to give the cube root of numbers in the hundreds of millions the very moment when it was asked. Somebody asked him once how many minutes there were in 48 years, he answered, 25,288,800.

Mozart, the great musician, wrote a sonata when he was four years old and an opera in his eighth year. Theresa Milanolla played the violin with such skill that many people thought that she must have played before her birth. There are many such instances of wonderful powers exhibited by artists and painters when they were quite young. Sankaracharya, the great commentator of the Vedanta philosophy, finished his commentary when he was twelve years old. How can such cases be explained by the theory of hereditary transmission? Many of you have heard of the wonderful musical talents of Blind Tom. This blind negro slave was born on his master's plantation and was brought up as a typical slave. He received no training in music or in any other line. One day when his master's family were at dinner he happened to come into his master's parlor and displayed his marvelous musical power for the first time by playing on his master's piano. Afterwards he was exhibited in different states of this country. Physically he was nothing but a typical negro. His intellect was very poor, but in music he was a master. His musical talents were so great that he composed music for himself and played his own compositions. Sometimes after hearing a new piece of rapid music once, he could reproduce it note for note. Where did he get all these powers? From whom did he inherit them? His parents perhaps never heard of a piano. He never had a lesson in his life, and he could not have understood even if he had had any. Not long ago I saw a girl of about six years, who played the piano most beautifully and who could reproduce the most difficult music after hearing it once. It seems to me that she must have played the piano in her previous incarnation. This is the only explanation that we can give.

Does heredity explain such cases? No. These illustrations are sufficient to disprove the theory of "cumulative heredity". "Cumulative" means gradualness. The believers in this theory say that a genius is the result of cumulative heredity, that is, it presents itself by degrees from less genius to greater and still greater and so on. In the whole history of the genealogy of geniuses, like Homer, Plato, Shakespeare, Goethe, Raphael, there never was in their families almost Plato, almost Shakespeare, or almost Goethe. Neither is it possible to trace the extraordinary powers of any of these back to any member of their ancestral line. Therefore we can say that no other theory than that of Reincarnation can explain satisfactorily the causes which produce geniuses and prodigies in this world.

Those who accept the truth of Reincarnation do not blame their parents for their poor talents, or for not possessing extraordinary powers, but they remain content with their own lot, knowing that they have made themselves as they are to-day by their own thoughts and deeds in their previous incarnations. They understand the meaning of the saying "what thou sowest thou must reap," and always endeavor to mould their future by better thoughts and better deeds. They explain all the inequalities and diversities of life and character by the law of "Karma," which governs the process of Reincarnation as well as the gradual evolution of the germs of life from lower to higher stages of existence.

98

EVOLUTION AND REINCARNATION

The amazing achievements of modern science have been opening every day new gates of wisdom and slowly bringing human minds nearer and nearer to the ultimate reality of the universe. The fire of knowledge kindled by science has already burnt down many dogmas and beliefs, held sacred by the superstition of the past, which stood in the way of truth seeking minds. In the first place science has disproved the theory of the creation of the universe out of nothing by the action of some supernatural power. It has shown that the universe did not appear in its present form or come into existence all of a sudden only a few thousand years ago, but that it has taken ages to pass through different stages before it could reach its present condition. Each of these stages was directly related to a previous stage by the law of causation, which always operates in accordance with definite rules. The phenomena of the universe, according to science, are subject to evolution, or gradual change and progressive development from a relatively uniform condition to a relative complexity. From the greatest solar system down to the smallest blade of grass, everything in the universe has taken its present shape and form through this cosmic process of evolution. Our planet earth has gradually evolved, perhaps out of a nebulous mass which existed at first in a gaseous state. The sun, moon, stars, satellites and other planets have come into existence by going through innumerable changes produced by the evolutionary process of the Cosmos. Through the same process plants, insects, fishes, reptiles, birds, animals, man, and all living matter that inhabit this earth have evolved from minute germs of life into their present forms. The theory of Evolution says that man did not come into existence all of a sudden, but is related to lower animals and to plants, either directly or indirectly. The germ of life had passed through various stages of physical form before it could appear as a man. That branch of science, which is called Embryology, has proved the fact that "man is the epitome of the whole creation." It tells that the human body before its birth passes through all the different stages of the animal kingdom- such as the polyp, fish, reptile, dog, ape, and at last, man.

If we remember that nature is always consistent, that her laws are uniform and that whatever exists in the microcosm exists also in the macrocosm, and then study nature, we shall find that all the germs of life which exist in the universe are bound to pass through stages resembling the embryonic types before they can appear in the form of man.

In explaining the theory of Evolution, science says that there are two principal factors in the process of evolution; the first is the tendency to vary, which exists in all living forms whether vegetable or animal; the second is the tendency of environment to influence that variation, either favorably or unfavorably. Without the first, evolution of any kind would be absolutely impossible. But the cause of that innate tendency to vary is still unknown to science. Upon the second depends the law of natural selection. The variation must be adapted to favorable conditions of life; consequently either the germ of life will select suitable environments or vary itself in order to suit the surrounding conditions, if they are unfavorable. But the agent of this selective process is the struggle for existence, which is a no less important factor. Thus Evolution depends on these three laws: Tendency to vary, or variation, natural selection, and struggle for existence. Science tries to explain through these three laws the physical, mental, intellectual, moral and spiritual evolution of mankind. But the theory of Evolution will remain unintelligible until science can trace the cause of that innate "tendency to vary" which exists in every stage of all living forms.

If we study closely we find that man's "self" consists of two natures, one animal and the other moral or spiritual. Animal nature includes all the animal propensities, desire for sense enjoyments, love of self, fear of death and struggle for existence. Each of these is to be found in lower animals as well as in human beings, the difference being only in degree and not in kind. In a savage tribe the expression of this animal nature is simple and natural, while in a highly civilized nation it is expressed not in a simple and straightforward manner, but in an artful and refined way. In a civilized community the same nature working through varied device, policy and plan brings the same results in a more polished form. In the struggle for existence amongst lower animals and savage tribes, those who are physically strong survive and gain advantage over those who are physically weak; while in the civilized world the same result is obtained, not by displaying physical force, but by art, diplomacy, policy, strategy and skill. Various kinds of defensive and offensive weapons have been invented to conquer those who are less skillful in using them, although they may be physically stronger. The simple expression of animal nature which we notice in savages and lower animals, by the natural process of evolution has gradually become more and more complex, as we find in the civilized nations of the world. The energy of the lower human nature is spent chiefly in the struggle for material existence.

But there is another nature in man which is higher than this. It expresses itself in various ways, but on a higher plane. Love of truth, mastery over passion, control of the senses, disinterested self-sacrifice, mercy and kindness to all creatures, desire to help the distressed, forgiveness, faith in a Supreme Being and devotion; all these are the expressions of that higher moral and spiritual nature. They cannot be explained as developed from animal nature by means of the struggle for material existence. For these qualities are not to be found in lower animals, although the struggle for existence is there. The moral and spiritual nature of human beings cannot be traced as the outgrowth or gradual development of the animal nature. There is a dispute among the Evolutionists as to the method of explaining their cause. Some say that these higher faculties have evolved out of the lower ones and have developed by variation and natural selection; while others hold that some other higher influence, law or agency is required to account for them.

Professor Huxley says: "As I have already urged, the practice of that which is ethically best- what we call goodness or virtue--involves a course of conduct which in all respects is opposed to that which leads to success in the cosmic struggle for existence. In place of ruthless self-assertion, it demands self-restraint; in place of thrusting aside or treading down all competitors, it requires that the individual shall not merely respect, but shall help his fellows; its influence is directed not so much to the survival of the fittest as to the fitting of as many as possible to survive. It repudiates the gladiatorial theory of existence. It demands that each man who enters into the enjoyment of the advantages of a polity shall be mindful of his debt to those who have laboriously constructed it, and shall take heed that no act of his weakens the fabric in which he has been permitted to live. Laws and moral precepts are directed to the end of curbing the cosmic process, and reminding the individual of his duty to the community, to the protection and influence of which he owes, if not existence itself, at least the life of something better than a brutal savage."

Prof. Calderwood says: "So far as human organism is concerned, there seem no overwhelming obstacles to be encountered by an evolution theory, but it seems impossible under such a theory to account for the appearance of the thinking, self-regulating life distinctly human." Thus, according to some of the best thinkers, the explanation of the moral and spiritual nature of man as a development of the animal nature, is quite insufficient and unsatisfactory. The theory of natural selection in the struggle for existence cannot explain the cause of the higher nature of man. We cannot say that a theory is complete because it explains many facts. On the contrary, if it fails to explain a single fact, then it is proved to be incomplete. As such, the theory that cannot explain satisfactorily the cause of the moral and spiritual nature of man cannot be accepted as a complete theory. That explanation will be considered as complete which will explain most satisfactorily all the various manifestations of the animal, moral and spiritual nature. Moreover, supposing the "tendency to vary" has evolved into the moral and spiritual nature of man, science does not explain the cause of that tendency to vary, nor how animal nature can be transformed into moral and spiritual nature. Is that "tendency to vary" indefinite, or is it limited by any definite law? Science does not say anything about it.

The explanation of the theologians, that the spiritual nature has been superadded to the animal nature by some extra cosmic spiritual agency is not scientific, nor does it appeal to our reason. Now let us see what Vedanta has to say on this point. Vedanta accepts evolution and admits the laws of variation and natural selection, but goes a step beyond modern science by explaining the cause of that "tendency to vary." It says, "there is nothing in the end which was not also in the beginning." It is a law which governs the process of evolution as well as the law of causation. If we admit this grand truth of nature, then it will not be difficult to explain by the theory of Evolution the gradual manifestation of the higher nature of man. The tendency of scientific monism is towards that end.

Some of the modern scientists who hold the monistic position have found out the same truth which was discovered long ago by the Vedantic philosophers in India. J. Arthur Thomson, an eminent English scientist of the present day, in his book on "The Study of Animal Life," says: "The world is one, not two-fold, the spiritual influx is the primal reality and there is nothing in the end which was not also in the beginning." But the evolutionists do not accept this truth. Let us understand it clearly. It means that that which existed potentially at the time of the beginning of evolution has gradually manifested in the various stages and grades of evolution. If we admit that a unicellular germ of life or a bioplasm, after passing through various stages of evolution, has ultimately manifested in the form of a highly developed human being, then we shall have to admit the potentiality of all the manifested powers in that germ or bioplasm, because the law is "that which exists in the end existed also in the beginning." The animal nature, higher nature, mind, intellect, spirit, all these exist potentially in the germ of life. If we do not admit this law then the problem will arise: How can non-existence become existent? How can something come out of nothing? How can that come into existence which did not exist before? Each germ of life, according to Vedanta, possesses infinite potentialities and infinite possibilities. The powers that remain latent have the natural tendency to manifest perfectly and to become actual. In their attempt they vary according to the surrounding environments, selecting suitable conditions or remaining latent as long as circumstances do not favor them. Therefore variation, according to Vedanta, is caused by this attempt of the potential powers to become actual. When life and mind began to evolve, the possibilities of action and reaction hitherto latent in the germ of

103

life became real and all things became, in a sense, new. Nobody can imagine the amount of latent power which a minute germ of life possesses until it expresses in gross form on the physical plane. By seeing the seed of a Banyan tree, one who has never seen the tree cannot imagine what powers lie dormant in it. When a baby is born we cannot tell whether he will be a great saint, or a wonderful artist, or a philosopher, or an idiot, or a villain of the worst type. Parents know nothing about his future. Along with his growth certain latent powers gradually begin to manifest. Those which are the strongest and most powerful, will overcome others and check their course for some time; but when the powers that remain subdued by stronger ones get favorable conditions they will appear in manifested forms. As, for instance, chemical forces may slumber in matter for a thousand years, but when the contact with the re-agents sets them free, they appear again and produce certain results. For thousands of years galvanism slumbered in copper and zinc, which lay quietly beside silver. As soon as all three are brought together under the required conditions silver is consumed in flame. A dry seed of a plant may preserve the slumbering power of growth through two or three thousand years and then reappear under favorable conditions. Sir G. Wilkinson, the great archaeologist, found some grains of wheat in a hermetically sealed vase in a grave at Thebes, which must have lain there for three thousand years. When Mr. Pettigrew sowed them they grew into plants. Some vegetable roots found in the hands of an Egyptian mummy, which must have been at least two thousand years old, were planted in a flower-pot, and they grew and flourished. Thus, whenever the latent powers get favorable conditions, they manifest according to their nature, even after thousands of years.

Similarly, there are many instances of slumbering mental powers. After remaining dormant for a long period in our normal condition, they may, in certain abnormal states--such as madness, delirium, catalepsy, hypnotic sleep and so forth-flash out into luminous consciousness and throw into absolute oblivion the powers that are manifesting in the normal state. Talents for eloquence, music, painting, and uncommon ingenuity in several mechanical arts, traces of which were never found in the ordinary normal condition, are often evolved in the state of madness. Somnambulists in deep sleep have solved most difficult mathematical problems and performed various acts with results which have surprised them in their normal waking states. Thus we can understand that each individual mind is the storehouse of many powers, various impressions and ideas, some of which manifest in our normal state, while others remain latent. Our present condition of mind and body is nothing but the manifested form of certain dormant powers that exist in ourselves. If new powers are roused up and begin to manifest the whole nature will be changed into a new form. The manifestation of latent powers is at the bottom of the evolution of one species into another. This idea has been expressed in a few words by Patanjali, the great Hindu evolutionist who lived long before the Christian era. [Footnote: The reader ought to know that the doctrine of Evolution was known in India long before the Christian era. About the seventh century, B. C., Kapila, the father of Hindu Evolutionists, explained this theory for the first time through logic and science. Sir Monier Monier Williams says: "Indeed if I may be allowed the anachronism, the Hindus were Spinozites more than 2,000 years before the existence of Spinoza; and Darwinians many centuries before Darwin; and Evolutionists many centuries before the doctrine of Evolution had been accepted by the scientists of our time and before any word like Evolution existed in any language of the world." Prof. Huxley says: "To say nothing of Indian Sages to whom Evolution was a familiar notion ages before Paul of Tarsus was born." In the second aphorism of the fourth chapter it is said, "The Evolution into another species is caused by the in-filling of nature." The nature is filled not from without but from within. Nothing is superadded to the individual soul from outside. The germs are already there, but their development depends upon their coming in contact with the necessary conditions requisite for proper manifestation. We sometimes see a wicked man suddenly become saintlike. There are instances of murderers and robbers becoming saints. A religionist will explain the cause of their sudden change, by saying that the grace of the Almighty has fallen upon them

105

and transformed their whole nature. But Vedanta says that the moral and spiritual powers that remained latent in them have been roused up, and the result is the sudden transformation. None can tell when or how the slumbering powers will wake up and begin to manifest. The germ of life, or the individual soul as it is ordinarily called, possesses infinite possibilities. Each germ of life is studying, as it were, the book of its own nature by unfolding one page after another. When it has gone through all the pages, or, in other words, all the stages of evolution, perfect knowledge is acquired, and its course is finished. We have read our lower nature by turning each page, or, in other words, by passing through each stage of animal life from the minutest bioplasm up to the present stage of existence. Now we are studying the pages which deal with moral and spiritual laws. If any one wants to read any page over again he will do it. Just as in reading a book, if anybody feels particularly interested in any page or chapter he will read it over and over again and will not open a new page or a new chapter until he is perfectly satisfied with it. Similarly, in reading the book of life, if the individual soul likes any particular stage, he will stay there until he is perfectly satisfied with it; after that he will go forward and study other pages. One may read very slowly, and another very fast; but whether we read slowly or rapidly each one of us is bound to read the whole book of nature and attain to perfection sooner or later.

According to Vedanta, the end and aim of Evolution is the attainment of perfection. Physical evolution of animal life reached its perfection in human form. There cannot be any other form higher than human on this earth under present conditions. It is the perfection of animal form. From this we can infer that the tendency of the law of Evolution is to reach perfection. When it is attained to, the whole purpose is served. Do we see in nature any other higher form evolved out of the human body? No. Shall we not be justified if we say that the end of physical evolution is the attainment of the perfection of animal form? Again as the purpose and method of natural laws are uniform throughout the universe, the end of intellectual, moral and spiritual evolution will be attained when intellectual, moral and spiritual perfection are

106

acquired. Intellectual perfection means perfection of intellect; and intellect is perfect when we understand the true nature of things and never mistake the unreal for the real, matter for spirit, non-eternal for eternal, or vice versa. Moral perfection consists in the destruction of selfishness; and spiritual perfection is the manifestation of the true nature of spirit which is immortal, free, divine and one with the Universal Spirit or God. Evolution attains to the highest fulfillment of its purpose when the spirit manifests perfectly. The tendency of nature is to have perfect manifestation of all her powers. When certain powers predominate they manifest first while the others remain dormant. As we find in the process of evolution, when animal nature manifests perfectly the moral and spiritual nature remain latent. Again when moral and spiritual nature manifest fully, the animal is in abeyance. It is for this reason we do not find expressions of moral and spiritual nature in lower animals or in those human beings who live like them. Man is the only animal in whom such perfect expressions of moral and spiritual nature are possible. When the individual soul begins to study its spiritual nature, its lower or animal nature is gradually eclipsed. As the higher nature becomes powerful the lower nature dwindles into insignificance; its energy is transformed into that of the higher nature, and ultimately it disappears altogether and rises no more. Then the soul becomes free from the lower or animal nature. There are many stages in the higher nature, as well as in the lower. Each of these stages binds the individual soul so long as it stays there. As it rises on a higher plane the lower stages disappear and cease to bind. But the moment that any individual, after passing through all the stages of the spiritual nature, reaches the ultimate point of perfection, he realizes his true nature, which is immortal and divine. Then his true individuality manifests. For lack of true knowledge, he identified himself with each stage successively and thought that his individuality was one with the powers, which were manifested in each stage. Consequently he thought by mistake that he was affected by the changes of each stage. But now he realizes that his real individuality always remained unaffected. He sees that his true individuality shines always in the same manner, although the limiting adjuncts may vary. As the light of a lamp appears of different colors, if it passes through glasses of different colors, so the light of the true individual appears as animal or human when it passes through the animal or human nature of the subtle body. The subtle body of an individual changes from animal nature through moral and spiritual into divine. As this gradual growth cannot be expected in one life we shall have to admit the truth of Reincarnation, which teaches gradual evolution of the germ of life or the individual soul through many lives and various forms. Otherwise the theory of Evolution will remain imperfect, incomplete and purposeless. The doctrine of Reincarnation differs from the accepted theory of Evolution in admitting a gradual but continuous evolution of the subtle body through many gross forms. The gross body may appear or disappear, but the subtle body continues to exist even after the dissolution of the gross body and re-manifests itself in some other form.

The theory of Reincarnation when properly understood will appear as a supplement to the theory of Evolution. Without this most important supplement the Evolution theory will never be complete and perfect. Evolution explains the process of life, while Reincarnation explains the purpose of life. Therefore, both must go hand in hand to make the explanation satisfactory in every respect. James Freeman Clarke says: "That man has come up to his present state of development by passing through lower forms, is the popular doctrine of science to-day. What is called Evolution teaches that we have reached our present state by a very long and gradual ascent from the lowest animal organizations. It is true that the Darwinian theory takes no notice of the evolution of the soul, but only of the body. But it appears to me that a combination of the two views would remove many difficulties which still attach to the theory of natural selection and the survival of the fittest. If we are to believe in Evolution let us have the assistance of the soul itself in this development of new species. Thus science and philosophy will co-operate, nor will poetry hesitate to lend her aid." Evolution of the body depends upon the evolution of the germ of life or the individual soul. When these two are combined the explanation becomes perfect.

The theory of Reincarnation is a logical necessity for the completion of the theory of Evolution. If we admit a continuous evolution of a unit of the germ of life through many gross manifestations then we unconsciously accept the teachings of the doctrine of Reincarnation. In passing through different forms and manifestations the unit of life does not lose its identity or individuality. As an atom does not lose its identity or individuality (if you allow me to suppose an atom has a kind of individuality) although it passes from the mineral, through the vegetable, into the animal, so the germ of life always preserves its identity or individuality although it passes through the different stages of evolution.

Therefore it is said in the "Bhagavad Gita," as in our ordinary life the individual soul passes from a baby body to a young one and from a young to an old, and carries with it all the impressions, ideas and experience that it has gathered in its former stage of existence and reproduces them in proper time, so when a man dies the individual soul passes from an old body into a new one, and takes with it the subtle body wherein are stored up all that it experienced and gathered during its past incarnations. Knowing this, wise men are never afraid of death. They know that death is nothing but a mere change from one body into another. Therefore, if any one does not succeed in conquering the lower nature by the higher, he will try again in his next incarnation, after starting from the point, which he reached in his past life. He will not begin again from the very beginning, but from the last stage at which he arrived. Thus we see that Reincarnation is the logical sequence of evolution. It completes and makes perfect that theory and explains the cause of the moral and spiritual nature of man.

WHICH IS SCIENTIFIC- RESURRECTION OR REINCARNATION?

The students of history are interested to know where the idea of resurrection first arose and how it was adopted by other nations. If we read carefully the writings ascribed to Moses and other writers of the Old Testament we find that the ancient Israelites did not believe in the Christian heaven or hell, nor in reward or punishment after death. It is doubtful whether they had any clear conception of the existence of soul after the dissolution of the human body. They had no definite idea of the hereafter. They did not believe in the resurrection either of the soul or body. Job longed for death thinking that it would end his mental agony. In Psalms we read, "Wilt Thou shew wonders to the dead? Shall the dead arise and praise Thee?" "In death there is no remembrance of Thee; in the grave who shall give Thee thanks?" Again, it is said about princes and the son of man; "His breath goeth forth, he returneth to his earth, in that very day his thoughts perish." "The dead praise not the Lord, neither any that go down into silence." Solomon speaks boldly: "All things come alike to all; there is one event to the righteous and to the wicked, to the good and to the clean and to the unclean... as is the good, so is the sinner." "Go thy way, eat thy bread with joy, and drink thy wine with a merry heart.... Live joyfully with thy wife... for there is no work, nor device, nor knowledge, nor wisdom in the grave, whither thou goest." Again in verse 5 it is said: "The dead know not anything, neither have they anymore a reward, for the memory of them is forgotten." Solomon says: "For that which befalleth the sons of men befalleth beasts; even one thing befalleth them; as the one dieth, so dieth the other; yea, they have all one breath, so that a man hath no pre-eminence above a beast." "All go into one place; all are of the dust and all turn to dust again." "Who knoweth the spirit of man that goeth upward and the spirit of the beast that goeth downward to the earth?" There are many such passages which show clearly that before the Babylonian captivity the Israelites had no belief in reward or punishment, neither in heaven nor hell nor in the resurrection of the soul. Some say that they had a belief in a sheol or pit where departed souls remained after death, but were never resurrected. But when the ancient Jews were conquered by the Persians, 536 B.C., they came in contact with a nation which had developed a belief in one God, in a heaven and a hell, in the resurrection of the dead, in reward and punishment after death, and in the last day of judgment. Under the dominion of Persia, whose rule began with the capture of Babylon and lasted from 536-333 B.C., the Jews were greatly influenced by the Persian religion. They gave up their idolatry, gradually developed social organization and had considerable liberty. About that time the Jews were divided into two classes, the Pharisees and Sadducees. Those who adopted the religious ideas of the Parsees were called Pharisees (according to some authorities the word Pharisee was the Hebrew form of Parsee), and those who followed strictly the Jewish ideas, ceremonies, rituals and beliefs were called Sadducees. The former were sharply opposed to the latter in their doctrinal beliefs. They believed in angels and spirits, they expected the resurrection of the dead and believed in future reward and punishment and also in Divine pre-ordination. The Sadducees did not step beyond the bounds of ancient Judaism. They were Orthodox and very conservative in their views. They denied the existence of angels and spirits, the resurrection of the dead, and reward and punishment after death. In Matt, xxii, 23, we read, "The same day came to him the Sadducees which say that there is no resurrection." The Sadducees were fewer in number than the Pharisees. Gradually the latter grew very powerful and after the death of Jesus their doctrines of the resurrection of the dead, and of reward and punishment after death, and the belief in angels and spirits, became the cardinal principles of the new Christian sect. Thus we see that the idea of resurrection first arose in Persia and afterwards took a prominent place in the writings of the New Testament, and since then it has been largely accepted by the Christians of the Western countries. The Zoroastrians believed that the soul of the dead hovers about the body for three nights and does not depart for the other world until the dawn after the third night. Then the righteous go to heaven and the wicked to hell. There the wicked remain until the time of renovation of the universe, that is, the judgment day. After the renovation, when

Ahriman or Satan is killed, the souls of the wicked will be purified and have everlasting progress. The question was asked, "How shall they produce resurrection?" Ahura Mazda says: "The reply is this, that the preparation and production of the resurrection are an achievement connected with miracle, a sublimity, and afterwards also a wondrous appearance unto the creatures uninformed. The secrets and affairs of the persistent Creator are like every mystery and secret."

The Zoroastrians believed in the resurrection, not of the physical body, but of the soul, and that it was an act of miracle. Similarly miraculous was the resurrection of Jesus. Although Jesus Himself never mentioned what kind of resurrection, whether of body or of soul that He meant and believed in, the interpretation of the writers of the Gospels shows that His disciples understood Him to mean bodily resurrection and the re-appearance of His physical form. The three days remained, just as the Zoroastrians believed. The miraculous and wondrous appearance of Jesus before His disciples was preached most vigorously by Paul. In his Epistle to the Corinthians, Paul declares emphatically that the whole of the Christian religion depends upon the miraculous resurrection and re-appearance of Jesus. Although Paul said the spiritual body of the risen dead is not the same as flesh and blood body, still that important point is generally overlooked, and the result is the belief which we find amongst some of the Christian sects; that at the call of the angels, the body will rise from the grave and the mouldering dust of bones and flesh will be put together by the miraculous power of the Almighty God. Paul says: "But now is Christ risen from the dead, and become the first fruits of them that slept". He preached that Christ was the first born from the dead, that those who believe in Christ would rise as He did and that those who would not believe in Him or in His resurrection should not rise.

We have already noticed that the Parsees believed in a miraculous resurrection; that the same miracle became more definite in the case of Jesus; and that the Christian faith was afterwards founded upon that miraculous event. Both the Parsees and the followers of Christ did not mean by resurrection any universal law, but a miracle done by certain supernatural powers. They did not give any scientific reasons for such a miracle.

But modern science denies miracles. It teaches that this universe is guided, not by miracles as the old thinkers used to believe, but by definite laws which are always consistent and universal. There cannot be any exception to those laws which are uniform throughout. If resurrection be one of those laws, then it must have existed before the birth of Jesus; as such, how could He be the first born from the dead, as described by Paul. Conversely, if Jesus was the first who rose from the dead, then resurrection cannot be a universal law. Scientists would not believe in anything which is not based upon universal laws. Some of the agnostics and materialists have gone so far as to say that Jesus did not die on the cross, but his animation was suspended when his body was taken down from the cross by Joseph of Arimathea. When Joseph went to Pilate and craved the body of Jesus, Pilate marveled if He were dead, because it was only six hours after the crucifixion. Some of the modern physiologists are of opinion that temperate and strong men might live for several days on the cross. These heretical agnostics and skeptical scientists say that the body of Jesus revived after a few hours in the cool, rock-cut tomb, that he walked out of the tomb, went to Galilee and appeared before his disciples. Whatever the facts may be (nobody can now tell exactly what actually happened), it is clear that the scientists are not ready to take anything upon authority. They do not care to believe in anything because it is written in this book or that. They must have convincing proofs and a rational explanation of every phenomenon of nature. They want to penetrate into miracles in order to discover the universal laws that govern them. If they do not find any such laws, they will surely reject every event that is supposed to be caused by miraculous or supernatural powers.

The theory of a miraculous resurrection is attended with the belief that the individual soul does not exist before birth. The supporters of this theory hold that at the time of birth, the individual, being created out of nothing, comes fresh into existence. But science tells us that sudden creation out of nothing and a total destruction of anything are both impossible. Matter and force are indestructible.

Science teaches evolution and not creation, and denies the intervention of any supernatural being as the cause of phenomenal changes. The theory of Resurrection ignores all these ultimate conclusions of modern science. On the contrary, the doctrine of Reincarnation, after accepting all the truths and laws of nature that have been discovered by modern science, carries them to their proper logical conclusions. Reincarnation is based upon evolution. It means a continuous evolution of an individual germ of life, and a gradual re-manifestation of all the powers and forces that exist in it potentially. Moreover, the doctrine of Reincarnation is founded on the law of cause and effect. It teaches that the cause is not outside of the effect, but lies in the effect. The cause is the potential or unmanifested state of the effect, and effect is the actual or manifested cause. There is one current of infinite force or power constantly flowing in the ocean of reality of the universe, and appearing in the innumerable forms of waves. We call one set of waves the cause of another set, but in fact that which is the cause is the potentiality of the future effect and the actuality of a previous potential cause. The underlying current is one and the same throughout. Reincarnation denies the idea that the soul has come into existence all of a sudden or has been created for the first time, but it holds that it has been existing from the beginningless past, and will exist all through eternity. The individual soul enjoys or suffers according to the acts it performs. All enjoyment and suffering are but the reactions of our actions. Actions are the causes and the reactions are the results. Our present life is the result of our past actions, and our future will be the result of the present. The actions which we are now doing will not be lost. Do you think that the thought-forces of one life-time will end suddenly after death? No. They will be conserved and remain potentially in the center and re-manifest under suitable conditions. Each human soul is nothing but a center of thought-force. This center is called in Sanskrit, Sukshma Sarira, or the subtle body of an individual. The subtle germ of life or, in other words, the invisible center of thought-forces, will manufacture a physical vehicle for expressing the latent powers that are ready for manifestation. This process will continue until the germ can express most perfectly all the powers that are coiled up in its invisible form. As the doctrine of Reincarnation is in agreement with all the physical laws, so it is based upon psychical, moral and ethical laws. As on the objective plane the law of action and reaction governs the objective phenomena, so on the subjective plane of consciousness, if the mental action or thought be good, the reaction will be good, and the reaction will be evil if the mental action be evil, because every action produces a similar reaction, A good reaction is one which makes us happy and brings pleasant sensations or peace of mind, while an evil reaction brings suffering, unpleasant sensations, and makes one miserable. Thus Reincarnation makes us free agents for action, as well as for reaping the results or reactions of those actions. In fact, we mould our own nature, according to our desires, tendencies and works.

The theory of Resurrection, as commonly understood, does not explain why one man is born with a sinful nature and another with a virtuous one. It contents itself with saying as Luther said: "Man is a beast of burden who only moves as his rider orders; sometimes God rides him and sometimes Satan." But why God should allow Satan to ride His own creature nobody can tell. At any rate, man must suffer eternally for the crimes which he is forced by Satan to commit. Moreover this theory pre-supposes predestination and that the individual soul is fore-doomed to go either to heaven or to hell. St. Augustine first started this doctrine of Predestination and Grace to explain why one is born sinful and another sinless. According to this theory, God, the merciful, favors somebody with His grace at the time of his birth and then he comes into this world ready to be saved, but the mass of humanity is born sinful and destined for eternal damnation. Very few indeed receive the gift of grace and are predestined to be saved. Moreover, this doctrine tells us that God creates man out of nothing, forbids him something, but at the same time He does not give him the power to obey His commands. Ultimately God punishes him with eternal torture on account of his weakness. The body and soul will not be separated. He will not be set free from his body, because, if it be so, there will be the end of his suffering, which God does not like. All these sufferings and punishments are predestined before his birth. Thus, St. Augustine's dogma of Predestination and Grace instead of explaining the difficulty satisfactorily brings horror and dread to human minds, while the doctrine of Reincarnation teaches gradual progress from lower to higher, through ages until the individual reaches perfection.

It holds that each individual will become perfect like Jesus or Buddha or like the Father in heaven and manifest divinity either in this life or in some other. One span of life is too short for developing one's powers to perfection. If you should try to train an idiot to become a great artist or a philosopher, would you ever succeed in your attempt to make him so during his lifetime? No. And will you punish him because he cannot become so? Can a man who possesses the slightest common sense be so unreasonable? Similarly what would you think if God punishes a man because he cannot become perfect within a lifetime? It is a poor argument to say that God has given us free-will to choose between right and wrong, and we are responsible for our choice; if we choose wrongly we must be punished. The advocates of such an argument forget that at the same time God has let loose His powerful Satan to corrupt His creatures.

It reminds me of an old story. Once on a time at a certain place a prisoner was released and set free through the kindness of a tyrant. The tyrant said to the prisoner "Look here, wicked man, I give you freedom, you can go to any place; but there is one condition; if you are attacked by any wild animal you will be put in the dungeon and there will be no end to your torture." So saying he gave him freedom, but at the same time ordered his servants to let loose a hungry wolf to chase the man. You can imagine what became of the prisoner. Can we call this an act of mercy!

The doctrine of Reincarnation says that each individual soul is potentially perfect and is gradually unfolding its powers and making them actual through the process of Evolution. At every step of that process it is gaining different experiences which last only for a time. Therefore neither God nor Satan is responsible for our good or evil actions. Good and evil are like the up and down or the crest and hollow of a wave in the sea. A wave cannot rise without making a hollow somewhere in the sea. So in the infinite ocean of reality innumerable waves are constantly rising. The summit of each wave is called good, while the hollow beside it is evil or misery and the current of each individual life is constantly flowing towards the ultimate destination which we call perfection. Who can tell how long it will take to reach that goal? If anybody can attain to perfection in this life, he is no longer bound to reincarnate. If he fails he will continue to progress by taking some other body. Reincarnation does not teach, as many people think, that in the next incarnation one will begin from the very beginning, but it says that one will start from that point which one reaches before death and will keep the thread of progress unbroken. It does not teach that we go back to animal bodies after death, but that we get our bodies according to our desires, tendencies and powers. If any person has no desire to come back to this world or to any other and does not want to enjoy any particular object of pleasure, and if he is perfectly free from selfishness that person will not have to come back. The theory of Reincarnation is logical and satisfactory. While the theory of Resurrection is neither based on scientific truths nor can it logically explain the cause of life and death, Reincarnation solves all the problems of life and explains scientifically all the questions and doubts that arise in the human mind.

"Reincarnation is not easily understood by a thoughtless child deluded by the delusion of wealth, name or fame. Everything ends with death, he thinks, and thus falls again and again under the sway of death."

THEORY OF TRANSMIGRATION

The theory of transmigration is one of the oldest theories accepted by the people of the Orient to solve the problems concerning life and death as well as to explain the continuity of existence after death. This theory presupposes the existence of the soul as an entity, which can live even when the gross material body is dead, or dissolved into its elements. Those who deny the existence of the soul, of the self-conscious thinker and actor, as an entity distinct from the gross material body, necessarily deny this theory of transmigration. The materialistic thinkers of all ages have refused to accept this theory, because they do not admit the existence of a soul or a self-conscious thinker and actor as an entity, separate from the gross material body. Consequently they do not ask or discuss whether the soul will exist after death or not, whether it will continue to live or not. Such materialists are not the creatures of the twentieth century, but they have lived in all ages, in all countries. In India and in other civilized countries of ancient times you will find that materialistic thinkers prevailed and they gave the same arguments which we hear now from the agnostics and scientists of to-day. Their arguments are generally one-sided and unsatisfactory. They try to deduce the soul or self-conscious entity from the combination of matter or material forces, but they have not succeeded in giving a scientific proof of it. No arguments in favor of the existence of a soul as an entity will convince them, because they deny the existence of anything that cannot be perceived by sense powers. If we could bring the soul down on the sense plane and make it visible to these materialistic thinkers, and if they could make experiments upon it, then perhaps they would be convinced to a certain extent, but not until then. But how can we bring the soul down on the sense plane when it is ethereal and finer than anything that we can perceive with our senses?

Those who try to explain the cause of our earthly life by the theory of heredity do not believe in the truth of transmigration. The modern scientists, agnostics and materialists generally accept the theory of heredity and endeavor to explain everything by it; but if we examine their arguments for the theory of heredity, we shall find that the theory of transmigration is much more satisfactory, much more rational than that of heredity.

Among the followers of the great religions of the world, the majority of Christians, Jews, Mohammedans and Parsees deny the truth of transmigration. Of course, there was a time when the Christians believed in this transmigration theory. Origen and other Church Fathers accepted it until the time of Justinian, who anathematized all those who believed in Reincarnation or the pre-existence of the soul. Among the Jews we find that in the Cabala this idea of transmigration plays the most important part. In fact the Cabalists accepted this theory to explain all the difficulties that could not be explained by any other theory. But those Jews, Christians, Mohammedans and Parsees who do not believe in the theory of transmigration accept the one-birth theory; that is, that God creates the souls at the time of birth out of nothing, and these souls, having come into existence out of nothing, continue to live forever; that this is our first and last birth that we receive; we did not exist before, we are suddenly created by God, and after death each one of us will continue to live either in heaven or hell to enjoy or to suffer throughout eternity. Among the modern Spiritualists we find that those who are born and brought up with this idea of one birth do not accept the theory of transmigration. Still there are millions and millions of people all over the world who do believe in transmigration and who have found comfort and consolation in their lives as well as a satisfactory solution of the problems of life and death.

The theory of Transmigration, or Metempsychosis, as it has been called by many philosophers, originally meant the passing of a soul from one body after death into another; or, in other words, it meant that the soul after dwelling in one particular body for a certain length of time leaves it at the time of death, and in order to gain experience enters into some other body, either human, animal or angelic, which is ready to receive it. It may migrate from the human body to an angelic body and then come down on the human plane, or to the animal plane and be born again as an animal. So the original meaning of transmigration or metempsychosis was the revolution of the soul from body to body whether animal, human, angelic or of the gods. The migrating substance being a fixed quantity, with fixed qualities, chooses its form according to its taste, desire and bent of character. This idea prevailed among the ancient Egyptians, according to whom the soul, after leaving the dead body, would travel from one body to another for thousands and thousands of years in order to gain experiences in each of the different stages of life.

Among the Greek philosophers we find that Pythagoras, Plato and their followers believed in this theory of Metempsychosis or Transmigration of souls. Pythagoras says: "After death the rational mind, having been freed from the chains of the body, assumes an ethereal vehicle and passes into the region of the dead where it remains till it is sent back to this world to inhabit some other body human or animal. After undergoing successive purgations, when it is sufficiently purified, it is received among the gods and returns to the eternal source from which it first proceeded." Plato also believed in this theory. Of course we cannot tell exactly from whence Pythagoras and Plato got these ideas. Some say that they learned these doctrines from Egypt; others believed that, either directly or indirectly, they learned the theory of transmigration from India. Plato describes in "Phaedrus," in mythological language, why and how the souls take their birth upon this plane, either as human or animal. He says: "In the heaven Zeus, the Father and Lord of all creatures, drives his winged car, ordering all things and superintending them. A host of deities and spirits follow him, each fulfilling his own function. Whoever will and can follows them. After taking this round, they advance by a steep course along the inner circumference of the heavenly vault and proceed to a banquet. The chariots of the gods, being well balanced and well driven, advance easily; others with difficulty; for the vicious horse, unless the charioteer has thoroughly broken him, weighs down the car by his proclivity towards the earth, whereupon the soul is put to the extremity of toil and effort. The souls of gods reach the summit, go outside and stand upon the surface of heaven, and enjoy celestial bliss. Such is the life of the gods; other souls, which follow God best and are likest to Him succeed in seeing the vision of truth and in entering into the outer world with great difficulty. The rest of the souls longing after the upper world all follow; but not being strong enough, they are carried round in the deep below, plunging, treading on one another, striving to be first, and there, in confusion and extremity of effort, many of them are lamed and have their wings broken. Thus when the soul is unable to follow and fails to behold the vision of Truth, sinks beneath the double load of forgetfulness and vice, her feathers fall from her and she drops to earth and is born again and again as human beings or as animals." Plato says: "Ten thousand years must elapse before the soul can return to the place from whence she came, for she cannot grow her wings in less." "At the end of the first thousand years, the souls of the good and of the evil kind come together to draw lots, and choose their bodies according to their tendencies and the bent of their characters. They may take any they like. Instead of receiving the natural consequences of their deeds and misdeeds of their previous lives they are allowed to choose their own lot, according to their experience and bent of character. Some, being disgusted with mankind, prefer to be born as animals, such as lions and eagles or some other animals. Others delight in trying their luck as human beings." From this mythological description we gather what Plato meant by transmigration.

This Platonic idea of transmigration or of successive lives of those who inhabit this earth has been criticized by various thinkers of modern times; and referring to this idea the late Doctor Myers, of the Psychical Research Society of London, writes in his second volume of "Human Personality": "The simple fact that such was probably the opinion of both Plato and Virgil shows that there is nothing here which is alien to the best reason or to the highest instincts of men. Nor, indeed, is it easy to realize any theory of the direct creation of spirits at such different stages of advancement as those which enter upon the earth in the guise of mortal man. There must, one feels, be some kind of continuity- some form of spiritual past." Why does He not create all souls equal? Why will one soul be highly advanced spiritually while another is entirely ignorant and idiotic? This question cannot be answered, this problem cannot be solved by the special creation theory, and therefore Doctor Myers says that there is no doubt that there was some previous continuity or spiritual past of each individual soul, and therefore he tacitly admits the theory of Transmigration. Although from a scientific viewpoint he could not give any direct proof regarding this idea of a pre-existence of the soul, still he could not deny it entirely when he said: "The shaping forces which have made our bodies and our minds what they are may always have been psychical forces- from the first living slime-speck to the complex intelligences of today." "The old transmigrationist's view would thus possess a share of truth and the actual man would be the resultant not only of intermingling heredities on father's and mother's sides, but of intermingling heredities, one of planetary and one of cosmic scope."

But this theory of Transmigration, as described by Plato, is a little different from a similar theory which existed in India before his time. In the Platonic idea of transmigration, as we have already seen, the souls were allowed to choose their own lot according to their experience or bent of character, but not to receive the natural consequence of their deeds and misdeeds. Plato did not say anything about the law which governs souls; but in ancient India the great thinkers and philosophers explained that each individual soul is bound by the inexorable law of nature to receive its body as a natural consequence of its former deeds and misdeeds, and not to have free choice of its lot according to its bent of character. The great thinkers and philosophers of ancient India discovered the universal law of cause and effect, of action and reaction, and called it by the Sanskrit term "Karma," which means the law of cause and sequence; that every cause must be followed by an effect of a similar nature, that every action must produce similar reaction, and conversely every reaction or effect is the result of an action or cause of a similar character. Thus there is always a balance and harmony between cause and effect, between action and reaction. This law of Karma has now become a fundamental verity of modern science. It is called by different names: the scientists call it the law of causation, the law of compensation, the law of retribution, the law of action and reaction, but they all refer to the same idea, that every cause must produce a similar result and every action must produce a similar reaction.

Now these ancient thinkers of India applied this law of Karma to explain the destiny of human souls, and it was upon this law they based the theory of Transmigration. They maintained that human souls are bound by this irresistible law and cannot get out of it; their thoughts and deeds are the causes which produce results of similar nature. So their future birth does not depend upon their whimsical, free choice, but it is limited by the thoughts and deeds or misdeeds of their previous lives. In the Platonic idea we find that the souls go according to their choice. They may not take a human form if they prefer an animal form, but in the Hindu idea of transmigration we find that it is not a result of free choice, but, if our thoughts and deeds force us to take a particular form, then we are subject to the law of Karma, which governs our future birth and the evolution of our souls. Consequently the Hindu theory of Transmigration differs fundamentally from the Platonic as well as from the Egyptian idea of Transmigration. In the Platonic and Egyptian theories we see that the souls, after leaving the body, enter into another body which is waiting to receive the migrating soul, but in the Hindu theory of Transmigration the body is not waiting to receive the migrating soul, but on the contrary the soul, being subject to the laws of evolution, manufactures the gross material body according to its desires and tendencies. Just as a germ of life will develop a grosser form by cellular subdivision, by growth, and by assimilation of the environmental conditions, so the germ of the human soul will manufacture the body by obeying the laws which govern the physical plane. Parents are nothing but the channels through which the migrating souls receive their material forms. Parents do not create the souls; they have no power to create. They can only give the suitable environments necessary for manufacturing a gross physical body. The souls come with their tendencies, with their desires, and they remain as germs of life.

Now these germs of life contain vital forces, sense powers, psychic powers, and ethereal particles of matter. At the time of death the soul contracts and withdraws all its powers from the sense organs to its innermost center, and in that contracted state it leaves the body. But these powers do not leave the soul. By the law of persistence of force and conservation of energy they remain latent in that center until environmental conditions become favorable for their remanifestation. Rebirth means the manifestation of the latent powers which exist in the germ of life or in the individual soul. These germs of life are called by different names. Leibnitz called them monads and modern scientists call them bioplasms or some such name, but the Vedanta philosophers describe them as subtle bodies. These germs or subtle bodies are subject to evolution and growth; they arise from lower to higher stages of development, from the mineral through the vegetable to the animal kingdom and eventually they become human beings and then they go on progressing.

In the Platonic theory the idea of progress, growth or gradual evolution of the soul from the lower to higher stages of existence is entirely excluded, because, as I have already said, the migrating substance is of a fixed quantity with fixed qualities, that is, these qualities do not change and are not affected by either growth or evolution. They are constant quantities. In order to differentiate these two ideas we should call the Hindu theory of Transmigration by the term "Reincarnation." The Hindu or Vedantic theory of Reincarnation, however, is not the same as the Buddhistic theory of Rebirth, for the Buddhists do not believe in the permanence of the soul entity. There is another point where the Reincarnation theory differs from Platonic transmigration. According to this theory of Reincarnation there is growth and evolution of each individual soul from the lower to higher stages of development. The soul or germ of life, after passing through the lower stages, comes to the human plane and gains experience and knowledge; and after coming to the human plane, it does not retrograde to animal bodies. The Platonic theory teaches that human souls migrate into animal bodies or angelic bodies and return from the angelic to the human or the animal, and that some of them prefer to become animals; while the theory of Reincarnation, taking its stand upon the scientific truth of gradual evolution, teaches that the human souls have already passed through different grades of the animal, nay, of the vegetable kingdom, by the natural process of evolution. After having once received the human organism, why should a soul choose to go back to the lesser and more imperfect organism of an animal? How is it possible for a lesser manifestation to hold a greater one? Why should a greater manifestation choose more limited forms in preference to those of others? This question arises in the Platonic theory of Transmigration. Therefore, the Reincarnation theory, or the theory of Transmigration according to the Hindus, rejects this idea of the going back of human souls to animal forms. We have already passed in the evolutionary process through the lower grade of animal organisms. Now that we have outgrown them why should we go back to them?

It is true, however, that in India there are many uneducated people among the Hindus who believe that human souls do migrate into animal bodies after death to gain experience and reap the results of their wicked deeds, being bound by the law of Karma; but in the Platonic theory the law of Karma plays no part in the transmigration of souls. The educated and thoughtful minds of India, however, accept the more rational and scientific theory of Reincarnation. Although there are passages in the scriptural writings of the Hindus which apparently refer to the retrogression of the human soul into animal nature, still such passages do not necessarily mean that the souls will be obliged to take animal bodies. They may live like animals even when they have human bodies, as we may find among us many people like cats and dogs and snakes in human form and they are often more vicious than natural cats, dogs or snakes. They are reaping their own Karma and manifesting their animal nature, though physically they look like human beings. This kind of retrogression is possible for one who after reaching the human plane goes backward on account of wicked thoughts and deeds on the animal plane. Such a temporary retrogression brings knowledge and helps it in its onward progress toward the manifestation of higher powers on the higher plane of consciousness. All the wicked thoughts and wicked deeds are nothing but the results of our own mistakes. What is sin? Sin is nothing but a mistake and it proceeds from ignorance. For instance, if I do not know that fire burns, I may put my finger into it and get burned. The result of this mistake is the burning of the finger and this has taught me once for all that fire burns; I shall never again put my finger into fire. So every mistake is a great teacher in the long run. No one is born so high and perfect as not to commit any mistake or any sin. Every mistake like this opens our eyes to the laws of the universe by bringing to us such results as we do not desire. As one life is not enough to gain experience in all the stages of evolution, we must have to admit the doctrine of the Reincarnation of the soul for the fulfillment of the ultimate purpose of earthly life. Professor Huxley says: "None but hasty thinkers will reject it on the ground of inherent absurdity. Like the doctrine of evolution itself that of transmigration has its roots in the world of reality."

For the most comprehensive selection of deeply transformative and healing Chakra Healing CD's and MP3's. visit
www.chakrahealingsounds.com

www.chakrahealingsounds.com
www.subliminalselfhypnosis.com

Made in the USA
Lexington, KY
19 March 2012